Never Forsaken
A Memoir

All Scripture quotations, unless otherwise noted,
are from the Holy Bible, Amplified Version.

All names have been changed to protect their private identity.

Interior design and editing by Gail Westerfield, Epiphany Writing and Editing
e.gail.w@gmail.com

Cover design by Lawanda D. Bethel
www.lawandabethel.com

First Edition: February 2013
Printed in the United States of America
ISBN: 978-1-62030-344-3

Never Forsaken

A Memoir

by

Takiya La'Shaune

With all glory, honor, and praise, I graciously give thanks to God, my creator and heavenly Father, Jesus, my savior and Lord, and to the Holy Spirit, my guide, help, and confidant. Without you, I am nothing, yet with you I am everything.

With just as much love and adoration, I thank my parents, family and friends for all that you have taught and contributed to my life, maturation and growth. Mommy, Daddy and Tiffany, I have never once stopped loving and praying for you and love you today, now more than ever.

To my spiritual parents, Pastor and First Lady, and the Life House Church family, I LOVE YOU ALL! Thank you a thousand times over for your prayers, love, compassion, hope, expectation, encouragement, and endless guidance. Your humbleness as a people of God and your hearts and minds like Christ have helped propel me to a place of faithfulness and obedience toward God.

To my dearest friend, Donyell, this book is lovingly dedicated to you. For many years, you saw the story within me, before I even knew it existed. Time and time again, as I weathered the storms of hurt, pain, and disappointment, you constantly encouraged me to write a book. You were never judgmental, always caring and reassuringly compassionate, even in times when I didn't love myself. The term "BFF" undoubtedly is an understatement to the true friend you have been to me. Here is your book!

Gail, my editor turned close friend, no words could ever truly describe my gratefulness for God placing you in my life at just the right place and just the right time. Your endless talents, effortless creativity, and immeasurable vision has helped to shape this memoir into the masterpiece it has become. Your patience and encouragement I commend, and for the bond that has been created, you will never be forgotten.

Lastly, and ever so importantly, are the blessings that God has added to my life. Nikole and Elijah, I love you with each growing day. My continued prayer is that God allows me to continue to cherish you as the gifts you are, to encourage you to be all that He has created you to be, and to know forever that He alone will Never Forsake you. Mommy loves you!

I was so honored to have had the opportunity to read *Never Forsaken* prior to it being published. Though I have known Takiya for well over ten years, have heard her story, and knew the ending, the book was hard to put down.

I am so glad that Takiya has been able to release all the hurt and pain of her past and is now able to move forward, tell her story, and contribute to helping others leave their pasts behind and move towards a happier, healthier future.

I have always viewed Takiya as an individual with a calling in her life to be placed on a level that most can only seek God to achieve. I have watched God deliver Takiya over and over, bringing her from nothing, again and again, while taking her beyond her mind's imagination. Takiya has a humble heart towards God and deserves all the blessings for her faithfulness and obedience to God.

For those of you reading this book, I admonish you to be patient in God's plan for your life. Love your sisters, mothers, friends, loved ones, and even those who seem to not love you at all. You may think you know an individual's story, but as Takiya has made compassionately clear, you may never know the whole story. The Bible, in the words of Jesus Christ himself, charges us to "love your enemies, do good to them that hate you, bless them that curse you, and pray for them that despitefully use you," (Luke 6:27-28 KJV) Issues, obstacles and hindrances from judgmental views and opinions of others may only further bruise or add damage to an already fragile individual.

Whether you are male or female, young or old, a Christian or not, look to God for strength to forgive and to be forgiven. If you are dealing with a painful past, have endured hurt, or can relate to any of the situations in Takiya's book, know that with God's help you, too, can be restored. Accept Jesus Christ into your heart and God will do for you just as He has done for my Sister and friend.

Takiya, you have always been a smart, beautiful and talented individual to me. I love you and am proud to call you my sister. I can't wait to see how God uses you and where He takes you!

– M. Joy
Spiritual Sister & Friend

"…I will not in any way fail you nor give you up,
nor leave you without support.
I will not, I will not, I will not in any degree leave you helpless
nor forsake you…"

– Hebrews 13:5

PROLOGUE

But all things are from God, Who through Jesus Christ reconciled us to Himself; received us into favor, brought us into harmony with Himself, and gave to us the ministry of reconciliation; that by word and deed we might aim to bring others into harmony with Him.

– 2 Corinthians 5:18

On January 12, 2009, exactly two weeks ago, I was given specific instruction to begin a journal of events in my life. This direction came from the bishop of a church that I had visited a few days after the New Year. I was invited by a friend to attend this event because the bishop was well known for his God-given ability to prophesy and accurately describe or discuss the past, present and future events of one's life.

I was a little reluctant to go, not because of skepticism, but because I was already a member of a church and was always a bit leery of the precision of others' teachings. However, I was persuaded to attend, and I later found myself not only in the church but standing at the altar, surrounded by most of the congregation. The prophet, Bishop Frank, had beckoned for me to come from my seat at the back of the church and spoke directly to me about the events of my life. Most of them were events that I had never shared with anyone other than God.

Bishop Frank spoke of how God had delivered me and kept me from my enemies and said that the trials of my past were all for God's plan for my life in Christ. He made reference to my newfound knowledge that I had struggled throughout my life with low self-esteem. He let me know that I was a queen, and that I should hold my head up high. He told me to move forward in God without the cares or weight of others upon me. He referred to the prayers of my mother and others for me and said that God was about to turn my life around and send me someone to love me *for me*. He told me that for my trouble and obedience, God was going to cause "the good measure, pressed down, shaken together, and running over!" which is a scripture based in Luke 6:33 referring to one's ability to be a blessing to others and having that blessing returned to them abundantly.

As I stood before the church and this man of God, tears streaming down my face, his final words were about this journal. He said the contents of this book would be a tool to be used as a testimony of God in my life. A tool to help women - perhaps millions of them - who had gone through or were going through what I had endured with life's struggles, low self-esteem, abuse, and so much hurt and pain.

Do I believe all of this? YES! Which is why, with obedience, I have sought the Lord for guidance and confirmation of this part of His plan for my life.

See, two years before this prophesy, my best friend, Donyell, constantly urged me and then God spoke to my Spirit and told me to begin to write a book. I was in the midst of a horribly unhealthy relationship that would soon turn into a powerful testimony of God's never-ending love for me. It was then that I became aware of the awesome power of God's presence in my life. All that He had brought me through needed to be shared. I had not endured and overcome such hardships on my own, and defying death more than three times wasn't just luck. I was here for a purpose, and God was showing me that it was time to begin the journey.

So Prophet Frank didn't just prophesy; he was used by God to confirm what was already apparently inevitable. God was telling me that it was time for Him to begin His ministry through me. It would be a women's ministry, as my life was a real life heroine drama come true.

How often we believe that pastors and prophets or apostles and evangelists are the only ones who are used to minister, to teach the Word of God, and to lead souls to salvation. Not so, as I am learning that God has many, many ways for each and every one of us to reach the lost, broken-hearted, desolate, deprived and depressed.

I truly, truly have overcome life's obstacles and let-downs by the words of my testimony, and it is with great honor, service, and obedience that I will pour out my soul and all that God allows me to share in this book. I pray that my life may give the name of my Lord and Savior Jesus Christ all the glory, and that I may be a witness for those to come, those who struggle, those who believe, and those who come to believe.

CHAPTER ONE

Before I formed you in the womb I knew and approved of you as my chosen instrument, and before you were born, I separated and set you apart, consecrating you; and I appointed you as a prophet to the nations.

– Jeremiah 1:5

My childhood and pre-teen years were probably no different than those of most girls in an average two-parent, middle class family. My mother was a stay-at-home mom, and I don't recall her working outside the home much until my sister and I were old enough to take care of ourselves. My dad is actually my sister's dad, my dad since I was about three years old. He was a career Marine whose position in the military allowed my mother to choose to work or to stay home.

To an inexperienced, innocent child, we all seemed happy, and there seemed to be no reason for our family to fail. Looking back on those years, I often wondered exactly how and when things in our seemingly solid family began to reshape themselves. We weren't poor, and we weren't rich. We always seemed to have what we needed and got what we wanted. My parents seemed happy; I never heard them argue or fight, and though my sister's dad was raising me as his stepdaughter, I never felt like he treated me as anything other than his very own child.

I was born in East Saint Louis, Illinois. We moved to the fast-paced, sunny state of California when I was about three or four years old. For me, growing up in the military wasn't so rough. We moved repeatedly over the years, and though I experienced the occasional difficulty learning about new places, making friends, and leaving behind old ones, I can't say that it bothered me much.

In Southern California, I was surrounded by all sorts of cultures, races, and nationalities, and it was there that I began to grow and learn. We spent about seven years in California before being stationed in a small town called Beaufort, off the South Carolina coast, when I was about ten.

I have very few early memories of Beaufort; however, I do recall that at this point in my life, things in my family began to shift. We lived in a cute three bedroom brick home on Linda Street, near the water. I didn't appreciate it at the time, but the views of the marsh from our home were spectacular. As kids, we took the beauty of things for granted, as we frowned and wrinkled our little noses up at the awful smell of the low tide as the water drifted up to the edge of the muddy shoreline. Our neighborhood was small and safe, and my sister Tiffany and I made friends with plenty of children who were both our ages. Friends of my parents, Mike and Lisa, lived a street over and we affectionately called them Aunt and Uncle.

At this time in my life, I felt safety, love, peace and happiness, all of which would slowly be taken from me.

My dad, because he was in the military, was deployed to other bases from time to time. When this occurred, my mother, Tiffany, and I would stay home and continue life as usual while my dad went off to another city or state, and, at times, another country. One time in particular, I vividly remember him having to travel to Puerto Rico. I was so sad that Daddy was going away.

Thinking back, it seems unbelievable that at one time I was a "Daddy's girl," and that we were as close and loving as we were. I missed my dad while he was away, and I remember a particular phone call to us girls from him, while he was in Puerto Rico. We talked excitedly and made sure to put in our requests for him to "climb trees and bring us back coconuts."

The night he returned home from Puerto Rico, Tiffany and I were thrilled. I remember both of us, so full of joy that Daddy was home, running to hug him when he came in the door. He lifted us both up in his arms for hugs and kisses. Immediately after, we grilled him with questions and petitions for our souvenirs.

Among the coconuts, as promised, were two stuffed teddy bears. One was a soft turquoise color for my sister, and the other was a dark shade of peach for me. They both wore little matching sweaters and had soft fuzzy fur.

We stayed up late that night playing with our new toys and rejoicing that Daddy was home. That night marked the last time I would ever feel sadness about seeing my dad go away or experience any happiness when he returned.

I don't remember exactly how old I was when I began to develop physically, but I don't think I had by this point in my life. The night my dad came back from Puerto Rico, though, some decision he made, or perhaps just an unconscious lack of judgment, led him to fondle me, completely out of the blue, for the first time.

That night, as my sister and I played, I noticed a difference in the way his hands were placed and the areas they touched as he would hug me. But because I was still an innocent child, and had never had talks with adults about "not-okay touching," it didn't occur to me to ask what was going on, let alone tell him to stop. He was my dad and he loved me, so everything was okay.

When my mom could finally get us to go to bed, my dad came into the bedroom. He went to Tiffany to kiss her goodnight first. As I lay there, I remember my dad walking over to my side and standing over my bed. He joked with me as he always did, calling me a silly little name as he leaned over to kiss me goodnight, but this time was different. As he leaned in, he slid his hand underneath my pajama top and rubbed my chest in circular motions before pulling away, standing up, and leaving the room.

I lay in bed, motionless and holding my breath, waiting for my dad to turn back and say something about what he had done. I finally went to sleep and never questioned that night. Thinking back on that moment now makes me cringe and shudder at the thought of him sliding his hands underneath my shirt. The shame of it added to my disgust, and though at the time I didn't know for certain that it was wrong, I repressed the memory, never speaking of it, until I was fifteen years old.

No one in our house ever talked about things like sex, puberty, boys, and right or wrong touching. I don't blame my mother because she only knew how to be what she was taught, and she probably felt no need or desire to give her girls that sort of talk.

I remember the day I came home from school because I had started my menstrual cycle. The only reason I even knew what was happening to me and my changing body was due to things my friends had told me. As a middle-schooler, I had not been given permission by my parents to watch a sex education video about puberty offered by the school nurse, and when I attempted to ask my mom about puberty, she quickly told me to be quiet because this sort of thing wasn't talked about.

The memory of that night seemed to fade away as quickly as it had appeared. I didn't speak up, not knowing that much later this silence would cause my confession to be rejected and considered a lie.

Ultimately, this revelation about what my dad did would send my family as a whole – as well as each of us individually – into a downward spiral.

YOUR JOURNAL

Thinking back on my childhood, and many times in my adult relationships, I chose to keep silent to avoid conflict or struggle, yet these were the times that my voice should have been heard the most. Can you think of a time in the past, maybe even today, that you have held something in for fear of being judged or not believed? How did it make you feel? What would you say and to whom would you say it, if you could?

In all of these journals, feel free to "free-write," which means to write for a designated period – 10-15 minutes or so – *without stopping*, while thinking about the questions I've posed. PLEASE don't worry about grammar or spelling or even your handwriting. This is a place to express your personal feelings and ideas. No one will grade or judge you. If you feel you've run out of things to say, just write about whatever's in your head at the moment and then go back to the topic. This is YOUR journal. Feel free to write whatever you'd like ... and to keep writing elsewhere when this section's pages are filled!

CHAPTER TWO

For I know the thoughts and plans that I have for you, says the Lord, thoughts and plans for welfare and peace and not for evil, to give you hope in your final outcome.

– Jeremiah 29:11

In 1990, when I was about thirteen years old, my dad received military orders to leave South Carolina, and we moved to Millington, Tennessee. Millington was another small town, about an hour away from Memphis. Entering the sixth grade, I attended Millington Middle School, and other than the usual pre-teen drama of coping with adolescence, boys, and wanting to be part of the "in crowd," my school life and education were average.

Home life, however, seemed to be taking a turn in a bad direction. I developed a sense of fear that soon turned to anger, and then hatred, for my dad. I no longer referred to him as my dad, but as my stepdad. I no longer cared to affectionately call him "Daddy." He seemed oblivious to the deterioration of our relationship and the lack of any father-daughter terms of endearment or gestures.

My mother, perhaps most of all, wrote this off as my growing up and just being rebellious, though the question of what was I rebelling against and why never seemed to arise. I was an above-average student, I never got in trouble at school, and I didn't know a thing about boys, kissing, sex, or relationships. I really didn't have many friends, and I was never allowed to go out.

At home – and, significantly, *only* when my mother was away – my dad was constantly putting me down and talking negatively to me. "You're a dummy," he would say. "You're stupid. You'll never be anything." "You're a tramp. You're a slut."

At 12 or 13 years old, I had no idea what a "tramp" or a "slut" even was. I had never even heard the terms, let alone committed the acts that would have merited those titles. I was clueless about what these venomous words meant or why he thought they were true of me. I built up such a hatred for my dad that I often wished that he would die.

I began to notice his pattern of picking on me when my mom was away and tried to keep hidden in my room or outside when I was permitted. I never tested his anger by talking back or standing up to him and kept my distance as often as possible in an attempt to ignore his crude, cruel ways.

My sister never endured such treatment, for which I was thankful. Not making the connection that my dad possibly resented me in some way for the molestation, I assumed that Tiffany wasn't mistreated because she was his "real" daughter. My real father wasn't very active in my life at all, and the couple of times that I had met him, he didn't indicate that he desired a relationship.

At times, Tiffany seemed to show compassion for me and was angry about the way I was treated. I remember standing in our kitchen one day, washing dishes. I was tired and in a hurry, so I wasn't washing them very well. Tiffany and I began to argue about it, and my dad, who was the only parent home at the time, yelled for me to leave the kitchen, then forcefully snatched me up and threw me to the living room floor. The act was so shocking, even to him, that he just looked wildly at me, as I lay there crying. Finally, regaining his composure, he spoke up and accused me of being overly dramatic, claiming that he had not "thrown me *that* hard." As he left the room, my sister came to my side to comfort me and help me up. Through her tears, she insisted that I should tell Mommy what he had done. Yet, like so many times before, I didn't let my mom know what was going on or how I was being treated when she wasn't around.

My mom seemed to have no patience with my dad's and my newfound and constant agitation with one another. He always seemed to find a way to turn my actions and innocence into those of a rebellious, ungrateful teen.

I was scared of him, and he knew it. His tough military background and uncaring behavior made it nearly impossible for me to ever get a word in that my mother would listen to, let alone believe, compared to her husband. He was the breadwinner of the house, the provider, and the "good guy." I was just a child.

Though I knew that the physical and verbal abuse was wrong, I still, even to this day, have an aversion to conflict. Perhaps I just wanted to keep some semblance of peace in our household. Maybe I felt that if I told my mother how he acted, it would break up their marriage and cause my mother and sister unhappiness. Who knows?

What I do know is that one by one, my family was turning on me and pushing me out. That day, there on the living room floor, is my last recollection of any sort of bond between my sister and me. We are so distant from one another that, even today, anyone who does not know us would never guess we were sisters or even knew one another.

I ran away that year. Not exactly on that day, and not exactly "away" either. One night my parents were getting ready to go to the annual Marine Corps Ball, and I wanted to go out with some friends. Of course, I was told I couldn't go, and I was furious. My sister, who was three years younger than I was, seemed to always get whatever she wanted, often exactly what *I* had asked for. This same year, she had been allowed to attend a *Boys II Men* concert with friends, while I was told that I couldn't, and for no apparent reason. I couldn't understand this, and in my frustration, my first true act of rebellion was conceived.

While my parents were getting dressed, I conspired to run away. I despised my dad and was irritated at my sister's growing knowledge that she could get more of anything than I could. Her father was teaching her that she was better than me because he was *her* dad and he was raising us. Though I never heard my mother support his words and actions, her silence only seemed to encourage this. My mother now seemed to be on the bandwagon with the two of them against me, since I had never spoken up, which allowed my dad further leverage against me.

Well, that night, rebellion is what they got. Without even packing any clothes or giving any thought to where I was going, I bolted out the front door. My heart was pounding as I raced across the front lawn, into the parking lot, and then into the backseat of my mother's 1987 white Plymouth Horizon: the very same car that they would probably hop in to drive around and look for me. As I ducked down behind the seat, I slowly raised my head to peek out the window at the house. "They'll miss me," I remember thinking, but I didn't care if they did. I felt so unloved; I knew they probably would barely notice I was gone.

I settled in, and with no game plan, just waited. About half an hour had passed when I realized that they had noticed I was gone, as I heard my parents and neighbors yelling my name. The neighbors sounded concerned, but my mother's voice sounded strained and frustrated. The reality of what I had done occurred to me, and fear set in. I contemplated *really* running away, but when I weighed my options, I knew that made no sense. My imagination was wide open as I realized how much trouble I was going to be in. This was truly my first act of genuine rebellion, and I had no idea how terrible a punishment my parents would come up with.

An hour or so after I'd run, I reluctantly climbed out the car and with feet like cement, walked back across the lawn into the house. I halfway hoped that they would be happy that I was safe and that I would be embraced – at least at first – but not a soul came to investigate the sound of the front door closing. Instead, I walked into my parent's room and was shocked to find them still getting ready for the ball. My mother stared at me with such disappointment and disgust.

"You've made us late for the ball," she said, "and now we might not be able to win a television set. Go to your room."

My dad never looked at me or said a word. I was later grounded for an undetermined length of time. Looking back now, grounding was an ironic joke, as every day of my life already seemed to be a punishment. I was never allowed to go anywhere, talk on the phone, or hang out with friends. When he felt like it, my dad would let me go out to play with the neighborhood kids, but most days, it was only my sister who was allowed to go out while I was made to stay in the house and do chores or read. I suppose my mother's demand that I go to my room was just about all that was left to be done to me.

My dad never said a word to me that night. In fact, he pretty much stopped talking to me at all unless it was necessary. For me, his silent treatment was welcomed bliss. I didn't want to talk to him, and I didn't want him talking to me either. His ignoring me allowed my imagination and wishes for him to be dead and disappear all the more attainable. I played right along with his game and would often walk into a room and cheerfully speak to my mother and Tiffany as if they were the only ones there.

However, my dad, not to be outdone, took his abuse toward me to a higher level of degradation. Soon, they began to leave me out of family events like going out to dinner or shopping. I was made to stay at home alone, and oftentimes my dad and Tiffany would come back bragging about their outings.

My mom never spoke up on my behalf. She just went along with my dad's mockery and immature antics, though his behavior was debilitating to my self-esteem and sense of who I was. My ego and emotions became so easy to bruise that I cried at the slightest insinuation of criticism, even if it was constructive. I even questioned my self-worth, and viewed myself as ugly.

I gained complex after complex about myself, even regarding my dark brown skin color. One day, my mother jokingly called me "Darkie," and I immediately burst into tears. She, as well, was now crippling me with demeaning comments about my looks, which was more than I could handle.

However, that day I realized something about my mother, as she immediately rushed to hug me and apologize through tears of her own. She said she had not meant to hurt me with her comment, and she showed the compassion a mother should give a daughter. I knew then that my mom loved me, and that the way I was being treated didn't sit well with her. I could guess that she had turned her back to some of the things my dad and sister did for reasons similar to my own: she didn't want to lose her marriage and stability.

YOUR JOURNAL

When we can learn to love ourselves, it is only then that we can love others. Perhaps there is someone in your life, such as a parent, friend or loved one, that constantly hurts you with words or actions. Could it be that the source of their lack of love for you stems from their lack of love for themselves? How does it make you feel to be attacked?

CHAPTER THREE

God sent me before you to preserve for you a posterity and to continue a remnant on the earth, to save your lives by a great escape and save for you many survivors.
So now it was not you who sent me here, but God...
– Genesis 45:7-8

Other than my botched attempt to run away, thus causing a new stage of separation in the family, life in Tennessee at that point was about as stable and calm as my life ever could be. Looking back, I realize the irony of that, because I see now that it was anything *but* stable.

Halfway through my freshman year of high school, we relocated back to Southern California, right off the Pacific Coast in Mission Viejo, near San Juan Capistrano. I loved it there. I quickly made a couple of close friends, and though we were not among the most popular girls, we had shared interests and formed our own little clique. Asia, my closest friend, and I bonded over the fact that now, at the age of 16, neither of us had ever been kissed, ever had boyfriends and were still virgins.

Looking back on it now, this innocence that I still had was completely twisted in my dad's eyes. He had no clue who I was. I couldn't understand what terrible thing I had done to cause him to treat me the way he did. The memory of what had happened the night he came home from Puerto Rico had long vanished. Even if the thought had resurfaced, I don't know if I could have made a connection between what he did then and the way he had treated me since that night.

Late one evening in my sophomore year, the memory somehow resurfaced. I remember having gotten in trouble for taking one of my dad's jackets without his permission. I can still remember the jacket. It was navy blue with an elastic band right below the waistline. It had two pockets on either side of the zipper, and they fastened with Velcro. I wanted to wear it to stash make-up, which I wasn't allowed to wear, in all of the pockets. I usually walked home, and at a certain point, I would stop and clean the makeup off my face.

This particular day, my mother met me before I got to that point. A boy I liked was walking with me, and as I stopped, shocked and bracing myself for the embarrassment, my mom let me have it! She was so upset with me that she snatched me by the collar of my jacket and pulled me all the way home. During the swift remainder of that walk, my mother complained about my behavior, saying how rebellious I was, and for no apparent reason.

At home, I nervously waited for my dad's arrival from work because I knew he would be angry, especially with a boy involved. He didn't disappoint my expectations. He didn't call me names but insinuated that I was having or was about to have sex. I got yelled at about the jacket and placed on punishment.

I knew taking the jacket and sneaking makeup was wrong, but I'd had enough of him falsely calling me a "slut." Reaching my boiling point, I yelled and screamed and cried so fiercely that my mom had to calm me down. It was the first time that I would tell my dad that I hated him, and I meant it. For every mean name that he had ever called me, I yelled venomously back at him. I called him stupid. I called him ignorant. I told him he wasn't my real dad.

At some point, he left the room, maybe even the house, and my mom and I were alone. She was angry with me, but she didn't yell. There was a counter in our kitchen that had bar stools around it, and I recall sitting on one of the stools as my mother was standing on the opposite side in the kitchen. She asked me what was wrong and why I disliked my dad so much.

Fuming, I asked myself the same question, only I knew the answers. "Look at how he treats me," I thought. "And why? What did I do?" I wasn't a terrible kid. I went to school, I made decent grades, I didn't curse, drink or smoke, and I didn't have a boyfriend or even date. Yes, I liked boys, but I was so shy and inexperienced that I had even avoided the ones who liked me.

As I sat at that counter, tuning out my mother's pleas, my mind went back in time. Where did all this start? What did I do? Why don't we get along? Why does he call me those names? Does he really think I am that way?

Then suddenly I remembered. Just as calmly as the thought had entered my mind, it crossed my lips into my mother's ears: "He touched me when I was little." My mother was fidgeting with the dial on the small portable TV/radio set on the counter when she heard me. Ironically enough, it was the same set they had almost lost in a raffle, for being late to the ball the night I had "run away."

She froze at the TV as our eyes met. Tears silently rolled down my cheeks as the thought of that night came slamming full force back into the forefront of my memory.

My mother was silent and stiff, still in mid-pose, for what seemed like forever, before she composed herself and tensely asked me what I had just said. Now through uncontrollable tears, I gasped for air, and hysterically repeated myself. I don't know how long this went on, but at some point – I suppose after my mother had had enough – she bellowed, "You watch too much TV! Too much *Beverly Hills 90210*!"

My crying intensified as I pleaded with my mom to believe me. Instead, I was sent to my room to begin a newly established punishment.

Hours must have passed as I sat in my room, feeling numb from the combined shock of my resurfacing memory and the slap in the face of my mother's words: "Your dad always said you were a liar." She had spat those words out as I walked away from the kitchen counter and to my room, silently shutting the door.

It was dark before I heard any signs of movement or conversation in the house. Finally, I heard muffled voices coming from my parents' room across the hall. I sat on the floor and pressed my ear to the door, recognizing that my dad wasn't quite shouting but was speaking harshly to my mom. I cracked my door open to peek out into the hallway. The double door entry to their bedroom was slightly ajar, probably unintentionally, but I remember the door jamb was faulty and would never catch quite right.

I eased out into the hallway, just enough to realize that the shower was running, and the conversation was coming from within their master bathroom. I felt I had a right to know what was going on. I remained hopeful that my mom was speaking up for me and had believed me after all.

Boldly, I pushed open the door to their room. My heart was racing as I prepared to confront my dad alongside my mom and defend her from any unjust words. Yet, as quickly as that adrenaline rose up in my veins, it was immediately doused. As I drew near the bathroom, I could hear that my dad's harsh tone had now melted into somber, pathetic tears. He sobbed about how much he had done for our family, how much he had given us, and how he loved me like I was his own child. How could she believe he would do such a thing? He ended all of this by telling my silent mother that she could believe him or believe me, and if she believed me, we could pack our things and go.

I turned to go back to my room, not needing to hear her decision, as her silence was the same as if she had yelled it. I knew what I needed to know.

For months afterwards, I lived in a bubble, floating through my days. I went to school, came home, and went straight to my room. My stepfather and I never talked, my mother and I rarely spoke, and my sister, about thirteen at the time, seemed oblivious to any of it. She had her friends, her life, and all of my things that were taken from me during my punishment. And she had "*her* dad," as she had begun to possessively call him. Little did she know that I couldn't have cared less and was glad that he wasn't *my* dad.

Late one afternoon, I came home from school and crossed paths with him leaving the house. He was sweaty and looked nervous. Maybe he was just surprised I was home. We didn't speak, but as my eyes met his when we passed, my heart began to race in fear. My sister was always home before me, and neither of my parents' work schedules ever permitted them to be home at this hour. What was he doing here with her? I ran into the house, my voice trembling as I yelled my little sister's name.

The image of him walking past me, fidgeting with his belt buckle, loomed largely in my mind. I wanted to vomit at the thought of what could have happened. I screamed my sister's name again as I swung open her bedroom door.

"What?!" she shouted. She was sitting at her desk, fully clothed and irritated with me for bursting in on her. I quickly scanned her, then her room, looking for any sign on her face or body that would implicate my dad, but finding nothing, I silently closed her door.

In my room, I sat on the floor and cried. The thought had never occurred to me before that she could have been "touched" as well. The idea scared and angered me. So that day, topping the list of words to describe my terrible emotional state, paranoia was added.

Had the thought that my sister might have been abused entered my mother's mind? How could she be so unconcerned about her children? Is she crazy? I couldn't come up with an answer to any of the questions. I did know that if my mother didn't have enough sense to think about these things, paranoid or not, I wouldn't allow my dad an opportunity to hurt my sister.

I began to hover around Tiffany in any way I possibly could, even inviting her into my room, or laying in her bed to watch TV late into the night until we both fell asleep, so that she wasn't alone. She had no clue what I was doing, and I never felt close enough to her or confident enough to talk to her about the past.

I did, however, start to talk to her about boys, probing to see what she knew, in an effort to search for any small detail that would suggest a history of abuse with her as well. I guess I finally got myself to a place of satisfaction and security because nothing she ever said or did presented a red flag to me.

In the meantime, my dad and I grew further apart as his actions towards me became borderline psychotic, in my opinion. I remember standing in my room late one night with the window blinds open. I wasn't concerned about my privacy, because my bedroom window faced our courtyard, which was fenced to block all outside view. Out of the corner of my eye, I noticed movement outside the window in the dark. I turned and peered out the window, only to see my dad standing, hands in his pockets, nonchalantly staring back at me.

My hands shook as I rushed to close my blinds, then ran across the room to lock my bedroom door. Completely shaken up, I sat on the floor, watching my door for hours. No one ever came and no words were ever spoken about that night.

What *was* that? *Was he crazy*? How long had he been watching me? Was he remorseful and didn't know how to approach me?

The answer to those questions came late one night as I came home from babysitting for my parents' friends, the Miller's, who lived a few houses up the street from us. I can still remember their youngest daughter, Arielle, a tomboy who was missing her front teeth.

I walked into our house, quietly locking the door. It was late, and I didn't want to disturb anyone. To my surprise, my dad was still up, sitting on the couch in the dark. He had his head laid back, turned up towards the ceiling. He called my name as I came into the house.

"What do you want?" I snarled at him. He was mumbling, and he almost seemed to be in pain. I walked over to him and half-heartedly asked what was wrong with him. He began murmuring again, speech slurred as if he were drunk, and just as I began to back away, he sat up, extended both hands towards me, and grabbed my breast.

The room spun around me as I stood there in shock and fear. As he freely moved his hands over my body, my fear turned into rage. I forcefully pushed his nasty hands away, stepped back, and ran to my room, shaking and crying as I realized that he wasn't at all remorseful.

He was taunting me with his disgusting victory.

YOUR JOURNAL

As hard as it may seem, expressing your innermost secrets can be the very thing needed to set you free. Is there someone in your life who has physically or emotionally violated your trust? If you could say anything to them, uninterrupted, about your feelings, what would you say right now?

CHAPTER FOUR

I will confess and praise You for You are fearful and wonderful and for the awful wonder of my birth! Wonderful are Your works, and that my inner self knows right well.

– Psalm 139:14

As I was nearing age 17 and entering my junior year of high school, we moved from San Juan Capistrano, California to Irvine, California. This was the sixth time we had moved throughout my primary and secondary school years, and though I had never been considered "popular," I was able to transition and make friends. But thanks to my mother's and few peers' remarks about my darker-than-acceptable complexion, I never considered myself to be pretty. As a matter of fact, I viewed myself as ugly and wrote off the idea of dating boys.

Then one morning, running late for class, I rushed past the student center where most of us kids gathered to hang out between classes. A friend of mine, Kevin, began to shift my thinking about my looks. He was a star athlete on the varsity football team, and we had a few classes together, but I didn't think he had ever paid any attention to me. Yet that day, as I hurried to class, I heard an admiring "wolf whistle," and someone calling my name. I turned to see Kevin and several of his teammates staring at me with big, approving grins on their faces. A little nervous and confused, I asked him what he wanted as he approached me.

Somewhere between him calling me "sexy chocolate" and stating that he liked the way I "wore my dress," I uncomfortably thanked him and euphorically walked to class. My head was in the clouds as I replayed that moment from beginning to end, again and again, and as I did, it became clearer to me why that very same morning my dad had made such an issue over my wearing my new cotton and lycra jersey knit dress. He had complained that it was too tight, even after I had pulled and stretched the material from my body to show him that it wasn't tight. Though that wasn't enough to satisfy his complaints, I paid him no mind as I left the house, assuming that he just wanted a reason to be at odds with me.

The dress was blue and white striped, long and form-fitting. I had developed a "form" for it to fit, and apparently boys liked it. Putting on that dress that morning, I was purely clueless of the attention it would bring, as it clung to the curves on my body that I had previously considered as just me being fat.

That day, a new sense of knowledge and a boost of self-esteem had been granted to me. Through clothes, I began to gain attention and confidence that I had never known before. My rebellion against my parents had grown, and I went against them whenever I could by doing everything they said not to do. But I wasn't your average wild teen. I was subtle in the beginning, doing simple things such as sneaking to talk on the phone or pressing my luck at coming home a few minutes later than I was allowed to.

I wasn't testing my parents' patience, exactly, but somehow, the more I pressed for things to go my way, the less they seemed to struggle. This was especially the case with my mother, as she seemed to grow weary of all the years of arguing and fighting between us all, but mainly my dad and me. My mom's anger and frustration had turned to concern and maybe even to compassion. She began to let me experience more freedom, and I was finally allowed to hang out with friends. I suspect it was more out of fear that I would truly run away again and perhaps never come back. At one point, I even stopped coming home on some days, staying overnight at a friend's home, not caring that the consequences would be my mother's lectures or my dad's angry attitude.

That summer, I met Richie. He was 19 and had just moved to California from New Orleans to live with his brother, a Marine who lived on the base near my home. Richie was really average in looks and didn't seem to have a thing going for him, but I was infatuated with him anyway. At 17, I finally had my first boyfriend, and he showed me every bit of attention a girl could possibly want. We spent every day of the summer together, hanging out at the movies, talking late into the night, just making each other laugh. When there was no place else to go, we would hang out at his brother's house.

Thinking back on those days, I can't help but reflect on how innocent things between us used to be. For my part, at least, I had no knowledge about or experience with sex or even kissing. Our relationship was strictly teenage fun without the pressure of being physical. For most of the time that we dated, holding hands or hugging was the extent of our physical relationship. I honestly can't recall ever kissing him; my close friend's cousin was my first *memorable* kiss, and that was long after my relationship with Richie had ended.

So physically, things were the way I liked them. I don't remember discussing sex with Richie, but we must have because he knew that I was a virgin, and he was patient with me. However, at some point Richie lost patience with my innocence, and the matter of my virginity resurfaced. I remember being at his brother's house when he gave me instructions to go home while my parents were away at work, and he would come over to see me before they came home. To make it look unplanned and not out of the ordinary, my sister was home, so he would ring the doorbell so that she could answer and let him in, instead of him sneaking in and us getting caught.

Surprisingly, even though my sister and I were still distant, she and my mother seemed to like Richie, and he was allowed to come over. My sister never told on me if he visited when they were not home. We could always count on her to go into her room and close the door, so she could say that she didn't know that he was over and couldn't be implicated if we were caught.

When Richie came over this day, as usual, she did just that: went into her room and closed the door. Yet, for the first time ever, I snuck him into *my* bedroom and softly shut the door. I didn't know what I was doing as I watched him quickly undress. My heart was pounding and my whole body was shaking as fear overtook me. I barely knew anything about sex, let alone how to do it. From the little bits of knowledge I had gathered in conversation with friends, all I had ever walked away with was that the first time would hurt.

As I lay on the bed, Richie began to tug at my pants, but by the time he had gotten them off, I had decided that I wasn't ready for this. He was already on top of me when I attempted to rise up and tell him "No." For a brief second, he paused, looking me straight in the eyes, then just as quickly, he continued as if he had not heard me. I felt a sharp piercing pain, and as tears welled up, I squirmed to move away, but he never eased up until he was satisfied.

Pulling away from me, I recall him looking down at the blood in disbelief, looking back up at me with a sorrowful face and saying "Oh, you really *were* a virgin." He dressed as quickly as he had undressed, and without even looking at me, mumbled, "I'll call you later," as he left. That was the last time I would ever see him. And I never told a soul about that day.

During the first quarter of my senior year, right after that summer with Richie, I began to experience sharp cramping pains in my abdomen. I remember standing in the student center among friends and suddenly crying out, doubling over in pain. My mother was called, and she immediately took me to see a doctor.

I don't know why or what she suspected, but instead of my general physician, she took me directly to a gynecologist, with no questions asked. Now, as an adult, I am just realizing that my mother either knew or assumed I was having sex.

I was given my first uncomfortable, embarrassing gynecological exam. I was diagnosed as having Chlamydia, an STD, which I had never heard of. Even after being diagnosed, I had no clue what it was or that I had gotten it from having sex with Richie. The appointment was very hushed and grim. The doctor didn't ask me any questions and only spoke to my mother, out of my earshot.

Walking out of the office with the prescription in hand, my mother's silence matched my somber mood. Now that I'm the mother of a young daughter, I realize how she must have felt – devastated and disappointed – yet at the time, I was clueless.

Later that evening, I was feeling happy that I was going to get relief for the pain. I was also filled with a sense of joy for my mother taking the time to come to my immediate rescue.

As a matter of fact, it wasn't until the next summer, a whole year later, that I understood that Richie had given me a sexually transmitted disease. I was at a girlfriend's home, and her cousin was going on about this guy she was dating and how he had given her Chlamydia. As it turned out, that guy was Richie. I sat numbly as my mind zeroed in on what I had experienced a year earlier. I was disgusted and angry with Richie. Not only had he taken away my virginity so quickly and ungratefully, as if it were nothing more than a game to be won, but he apparently made a habit of having unprotected sex, which had exposed him to an STD, which he then passed on to me, this other girl, and who knew who else?

Even once the Chlamydia was long gone, I carried the private matters of my past well into my adult years. I felt burdened, unclean, scarred, used, and broken. At this point in my life, I felt certain that I only deserved to have one type of man. Due to my being molested as a child, then sexually assaulted as a teenager, I believed that I didn't deserve a meaningful, respectful relationship.

YOUR JOURNAL

There are times in life when we all may experience some form of self-doubt, whether by choices and decisions of our own or by actions toward or against us. Nonetheless, God does not see us as anything less than His beloved. He made you to be exactly who you are. What are things that you like about yourself? What are some attributes that speak positively to whom you are?

CHAPTER FIVE

But He said to me, My grace is enough for you;
for My strength and power are made perfect
and show themselves most effective in weakness...
– 2 Corinthians 12:9

After Richie, I had several friends whom I wouldn't necessarily call boyfriends, but I had begun to feel that sex was a necessary tool to use in order to get a guy. Then I met Eric, a 22-year-old Marine, whom I dated throughout my senior year of high school. I was now 18, and I often wondered what he could possibly have wanted from me, since I was four years younger than he was. However, he never treated me immaturely because of the difference in our ages. If anything, he treated me just as his equal.

He was my first true love, and the first man whom I knew loved me back. I could go on and on for pages about my relationship with Eric. He was wonderful to me. Of course, initially, because of his age and being a Marine, my parents were not thrilled, but this guy had staying power. He was respectful and honorable. He insisted on my being obedient to my parents' rules and instructions, even regarding my time with him. He was a gentleman.

My mom couldn't help but adore him, though my dad didn't budge too much. As a father and a Marine of higher rank, I suppose that was to be expected. We often argued about the time I spent with Eric. I was out of high school with no plans, and at Eric's coercing, I had made a sudden decision to postpone college, so my arguments with my dad always ended with a threat from him to put me out his house.

One evening I welcomed those threats and began packing. I had no idea where I would live. I called Eric, who lived in the Marine housing barracks on base. I knew I couldn't live there, but I also knew that he would do anything to see that I was taken care of.

My mom, who by this time was emotionally exhausted by the fighting between my dad and me, began to cry and plead with him not to put me out and for me not to go. I remember packing my things, her *unpacking* my things, and my dad repacking things. It was crazy! I had taken a lot out on my mom for her past actions, so I didn't feel any remorse for hurting her feelings by leaving. I was actually quite elated when I realized I was old enough to leave.

I packed everything I had, and by the time Eric showed up, I was ecstatic to be moving on to a new life. My mom talked to him, and he promised to take care of me. I sat in the car looking at them while she tearfully gave him a hug and waved to me. My dad was nowhere around, but had already told Eric at some point that I was now *his* problem to take care of, and I couldn't come back to my parents' home.

We moved less than five miles from their place, but I felt like I was in a completely different world. Eric had a friend and fellow Marine, David, who allowed us to move into a three-bedroom home he owned. The three of us living together worked out fine. David and Eric worked all week long during the day, and I worked second shift at a local hair salon chain, Fantastic Sam's, as the receptionist and shampoo girl. Life was good. It makes me laugh now to realize how, at eighteen years old, I was certain I was headed in the right direction. I remember these guys being my guinea pigs at breakfast, lunch, and dinner. If I could only draw a picture of their faces as I set my hard work on plates in front of them ...

Some days, I would call my mom or go visit her when my dad wasn't home. She would always tell me that my dad didn't mean it when he kicked me out and that I could come back home any time. I never thought I would, but after about 3 months, I did. Eric actually convinced me to go back. He had gotten orders to go to Japan, and as heartbroken as I was, he felt that I should live at my parents' for the year he was gone.

We were sure we would get married when he returned. According to Eric, being single in the military would require him to go overseas to Japan for a minimum of one year; however, if we decided to marry before he moved to Japan, he would be required to be stationed there for a minimum of three years. This was military protocol, due to the amount of effort and finances invested on its part to move an entire family overseas versus a single active duty employee.

So, at Eric's urging, I went back home to my parents, with a few months to go before Eric's scheduled departure. I don't know if he was anxious about our separation, but he became very possessive and distrustful. This had never been an issue in our relationship before, and initially, I didn't take him very seriously.

I had more male friends than female. Though my relationships with guys were all strictly platonic, Eric wouldn't accept my having male friends. I understood his concern, and for the most part I respected his wish for me to sever those ties. However, there were at least two close friends, Kevin and James, with whom I am still friends to this day. I kept these friendships a secret, rationalizing that what Eric didn't know wouldn't hurt him, and I wouldn't part with my friends – who were more like brothers – even for Eric.

One day, I began to see just how much influence Eric had over me. I was describing my relationship with Eric to Kevin, and it angered him to hear my complaints.

"He's too possessive, and I can't be your friend with him around," Kevin told me. But luckily, he was too good of a friend to really cut me off.

"He always thinks you're cheating" is a phrase I would hear about men in my life well into my adult years, and it started with Eric. Though I gave some thought to what Kevin had said, I finally just shook if off. He didn't understand: Eric and I were getting married, and he loved me. He was just jealous and overprotective because that is what men *did* when they loved you, I thought.

"Of course he gets angry and yells at me when other men are near me," I told myself. "Because he *loves* me." I can't tell you how many times I have replayed this time of my life in my mind and felt so naïve and just flat out dumb.

Jessica, one of my closest friends from high school, was celebrating her nineteenth birthday and wanted me to hang out with her for dinner and a night of clubbing. Against Eric's wishes, I went and ended up with Jessica and two of our male friends, Vick and Chuck. Knowing what could lie ahead if Eric found out, I only stayed through dinner and then had my friends drop me off at Eric's room at the barracks.

Unaware that Eric had seen all of us pull up in Jessica's car, I entered his room, only to find that he wasn't there. I left and walked down the corridor to the pool hall, which I knew he often visited. I peeked into the darkened room, and just as I turned to leave, I heard Eric call my name. A dim light at the back of the room flickered on, and I could see that he had been sitting there in the dark and was noticeably angry. He had been drinking, and his eyes were bloodshot. I will never forget his wild-eyed look; I have never seen another human being's eyes look so evil.

In all the time I had spent with Eric, I had never once feared him or felt threatened. That night, about six months into our relationship, was my introduction to fearing a man and what he could possibly do to me.

He terrified me, and as he began to approach me, cursing me and calling me names, he clutched a pool ball in his hand.

I backed into a corner and couldn't move. He got so close to my face that I braced myself for whatever was coming. Tears rolled down my cheeks as he grabbed my wrist and dragged me out of the room, pushed me onto the sidewalk, and slammed the door without saying a word to me.

I stood there shaking and crying until a car pulled up, which turned out to be my friends. Jessica jumped out of the car, yelling "I told you he's crazy! You need to leave him. I knew better than to leave you alone with him here!"

But instead of listening to her, I composed myself, looked up, and nervously told them to leave because I was staying. I pleaded for them to leave before Eric came out and started a scene. Vick and Chuck, who were like brothers to me, decided to wait downstairs while Jessica walked me back to Eric's room. I didn't hear a word she said on my way to the room. I fumbled around in my purse to find my key, and somehow convinced her to leave, reassuring her that things would be okay.

I don't know how long I waited in his room before he finally showed up. He didn't expect me to be there, and when he came in, he didn't say a word to me and wouldn't even look at me. I cried for him to talk to me, told him I was sorry, and begged him to forgive me and not to leave me. I was young, insecure, and in love, and I thought the things that he had done were acceptable. I thought that because I had not been entirely truthful with him, it was okay for him to treat me badly. Here it was: proof that Eric actually loved me and wanted me only for himself, and I was selfishly causing him pain.

I told him I was sorry and didn't want him to leave me. Eric said he forgave me, but I know now that he had also learned that my lack of self-esteem gave him a whole new level of control over me. I was like a dog on a short, choking leash. I was told where to go, what to eat, how to look, and what to wear. Eric had changed so drastically in the few months prior to his deployment to Japan. All he ever did was blame *me* for what *he* did, yet I was the one who had not changed at all. I don't know how I kept any of my friends, because even when Eric "allowed" me to have them, he monitored their visits, then found a way to find fault with them and run them off.

Later that summer, we gathered at one of his friend's room for drinks, games, and food. There were only four of us there: Eric, Jessica and her boyfriend Darryl, and me. Somewhere between drinks, games, and me acting in a way Eric felt was "inappropriate" with Darryl, Eric became angry and left. I didn't follow because I knew that he wanted me to. I knew that I had not done anything wrong; I was just talking to Darryl. He was my best friend's boyfriend, and we were all having a good time.

After about an hour, Eric still had not returned, so I went down to his room to check on him. As I neared the final flight of stairs, I could see Eric at the bottom of them, speaking to a female Marine. When I caught his eye, he was shocked and immediately urged her to go into her room. Confused, I gave him a questioning look and asked him what he was doing.

Instead of answering me, he went off on me about Darryl and asked why I had not come down to him sooner. This time, instead of answering him, I calmly made a statement: "You're cheating on me." It came out without hesitation as I recollected a conversation with Kevin, who had said to me that "no man is going to always accuse you of cheating unless he is doing it himself."

Eric walked over to me and grabbed me by the shoulders to shake me, but I jumped back and screamed, "Don't touch me!" I shouted it with so much force and anger that it brought tears to his eyes. I didn't even wait for a response as I turned and stormed back up to Darryl's room to find Jessica. Eric never came up behind me, and as much as I loved him, as much control that he had over me, as little self-esteem as I had to work with, I felt it was over. Deep inside, I knew that I couldn't deal with his cheating.

Back in Darryl's room, I didn't cry much. Jessica consoled me and then, after an hour or so, decided to take me home. Walking downstairs, we had to pass Eric's room. His door was slightly ajar, but it was well into the early morning hours. At first, I had no intention of speaking to him, but for some reason I stopped to check on him. I peeked in and could see him at his desk with a small light on and music playing. His head was on his desk, surrounded by alcohol bottles and empty beer cans.

Assuming he was passed out drunk, I walked in to wake him and to tell him to go to bed. I called his name and got no response. I tapped his shoulder, but he didn't move. Finally, standing over him and leaning in closer, I saw the blood and razor lying on his desk. I froze, imagining the worst; my chest started to heave, and I struggled for breath. I yelled his name and shook him, but he wouldn't move. I screamed and screamed, running out of his room and falling into the street, crying uncontrollably, yelling that he was dead.

Everything after that was a blur. Somewhere between me being carried out of the street, half the barracks being awakened, and the sounds of sirens, Eric was roused from his drunken stupor and given a good look-over by the military police. He was nothing more than drunk and "mentally confused." It turned out that he was trying to gain some attention and take the heat off of himself for cheating on me. To this day, I am not sure where the blood came from, because his wrists were not cut at all, as I had assumed.

Strategically propping open his bedroom door made no sense to me. Whether he had intended to go through with committing suicide or was just trying to get attention, I can't clearly answer. However, if it was his way of making me forget the break up and keeping me bound to him, he accomplished just that.

Of course, in my mind, I felt like he needed me. "How could I possibly leave a man who loved me so much that he was willing to take his own life if he couldn't have me?"

We never talked about that night, and for the next two or three months until he left for Japan, it was all about him. He took care of me, but I catered to all of his controlling needs. My relationship with him and my friendships competed until I basically had no friends. Somehow it didn't matter because Eric had made it quite clear that he was all I would ever need, and he would *always* be there. I believed him.

In Fall 1995, Eric left for Japan. Living back at my parents' place, I had plans to work until he returned. At Eric's suggestion, I decided to put my dream of auditioning for The Juilliard School, in dance, on hold. I was a dancer and had always planned to attend the nationally acclaimed school. All through high school, dance was my passion. I wasn't much of a scholar and only attended class because it was required. I barely graduated because I didn't take my education very seriously. However, dance excited and motivated me, and it was all I wanted to do.

My dad, of course, never encouraged that desire in my life and said that it wasn't a real career. He often related dance to "exotic" dancers and said it was only an occupation for strippers as he tried to corrupt the true art and beauty of my dream.

I had experience in ballet, jazz, contemporary dance, and tap. My senior year, as I performed in a talent show, my mother realized my talent and complimented me. I will never forget the day that she encouraged me and brought home pamphlets and information on Juilliard. I had never even heard of the school until then. But then my dream got lost in what Eric thought was and wasn't "best for me."

In June 1996, my father received orders to relocate to Beaufort, South Carolina. I was now challenged with the decision to stay on my own in California and wait for Eric to return, or to move to South Carolina with my family. Of course I listened to Eric, who thought it would be best for me to go with my parents to save money. I later found out that this was nothing more than a way for him and my mother to keep an eye on me. Yet, another way to control me.

YOUR JOURNAL

Psychologically, the mind needs to dream so that the body can continue to live. When we equate this analogy with our physical lives, you can see how important it is to attain, aspire to, and reach for our dreams. No matter who says you can or can't, don't stop dreaming. It is your livelihood and lifeline. What are your goals, dreams and desires?

CHAPTER SIX

There is no fear in love, but full-grown love turns fear out of doors and expels every trace of terror!
For fear brings with it the thought of punishment,
and he who is afraid has not reached the full maturity of love
– 1 John 4:18

I moved with my family back to Beaufort, South Carolina during the summer of 1996. It was a desperately hot, boring, small country town compared to the exciting city life I loved in California. The first things I noticed in Beaufort were that there was no mall, street lights, or sidewalks. There were always animals – squirrels, possums, or raccoons – dead on the roadside, and it wasn't uncommon for a family of deer to dart out in front of our cars with no warning. Miserable and lonely, I cried for two whole weeks. I had no friends and no job to even get out and socialize in the community.

For the first couple of months, the highlight of my day was receiving phone calls from Eric over in Japan, but soon that, too, was taken from me. My dad began to complain to my mother, who in turn complained to me, about the times Eric would call. The 14-hour time difference between Japan and Beaufort made for late night or early morning calls that interrupted everyone's sleep. At some point, Eric began to mail phone calling cards and cash so that I could call him, but my parents were displeased by this, too.

I was told that I could no longer use the home phone and would need to walk to the corner store to use the pay phone. With no other choice, I did just that, almost daily, late into the dark night or early in the still, dark mornings. I was terrified out there in the pitch dark – with only one street light over the phone booth, surrounded by trees and bushes – but if Eric had no way of reaching me or hearing from me, he would snap into a rage, yelling and cussing at me, questioning my whereabouts and the company I was keeping.

By now, after nearly a year of his derogatory and disrespectful words, I was actually used to it and expected it, but the fear that he evoked never seemed to go away.

Back then I didn't know it, but there was a drug house directly across the street from the convenience store where I would call Eric. Fortunately, no one ever bothered me, but I often thought about the fact that no one from my family ever bothered to check on me either. Little did I know, even though it wasn't family, *someone* was watching me.

I met "Q" coming out of the convenience store one day. He was tall, skinny, and thuggish looking. I remember thinking to myself, then actually telling him, that he was "the knock-off version of Tupac Shakur." Q was harmless, two or three years younger than I was, and new to Beaufort as well, having moved there from New York.

The first time I met Q, he hit on me, or rather attempted to express his attraction to me. He was quiet and shy, but what caught my attention was him mentioning that he saw me on the pay phone all the time. His dad owned the laundromat next to the convenience store, so they lived nearby, obviously close enough that Q had seen me coming and going. He said he had watched to make sure I was okay but never spoke to me because he could tell I was on the phone with a man.

I guess from that day on, Q became somewhat of a friend, since I had none. He lived in the neighborhood, so he was someone to talk to. He definitely didn't interest me romantically because I was only in love with Eric and had no intention of dating anyone else. Not to mention I was 19 and Q was only 16 or 17, but he kept me company. He liked me, and I knew it, but I had always made it clear that there was nothing there. I had even joked with my mom about his crush but had made it clear that he was just a friend.

Q was welcomed to come over and hang out on our porch with me during the day, but he was never allowed in the house, which was fine with me because this would keep our friendship clear and innocent. Or so I thought.

A month or so after I met Q, I went into the convenience store, and his father was there. He had a snide, disapproving look, which wasn't normal for him. Then Q came in, and I don't recall exactly what was said, but basically, Q told his dad that I was his girlfriend and that we were having sex, which was my reason for being out of the house so late at night.

I stood there numb, horrified, and enraged. I stared in disbelief at this nut who had not only lied about me, but was crazy enough to lie about me *right in front of me!* I couldn't say a word. I couldn't even cry. I just walked out of the store and went home.

Q followed me onto my front porch, and I snapped. I began screaming and cursing at him, telling him to leave and never come back.

My mom came rushing outside, yelling for me to calm down, and asking what was going on. I was relieved because I just knew that she was going to let him have it once she heard what he'd said about me. Through my tears, I began to tell her of his lies, and by the time I finished, I was pushing him and screaming for him to get out of our yard again.

Suddenly, my mother yelled, "Hey! This isn't your house! You don't pay any bills here! You can't tell people when to come and when to leave!"

Shocked, I watched as my mom ushered Q into our house for the first time ever. She asked him to have a seat and allowed him to talk. I sat in a corner and just cried as he told my mother the same lies he'd told his father. I didn't say a word; as if Q's lies were not enough, my mother told me that Q's dad had already added to this surreal event by telling my mom that he had actually "seen us."

I asked my mother when this conversation had taken place and begged her to explain to me exactly what Q's dad had said and when and what he had "seen." I even pleaded with her to invite him over so we could confront him as well. She just ignored my questions, disregarded my tears, and chose not to respond to my requests.

My mom repeatedly called me a liar, among other names, and questioned me over and over, claiming it made no sense for Q to lie about such a thing. I ended up going to my room and shutting the door, leaving Q and my mother in the living room. I lay on my bed and went to sleep to drown out their voices. I had no clue why Q would make up such lies, and even more perplexing, why his father, an adult, would join in with him.

It wasn't until about 10 years later, when I ran into Q in the local Dollar General, that I received an apology from him. He still looked the same, but what caught my attention was the Tupac Shakur style scarf still tied around his head, gangster style. Though I had long since matured and had forgiven him and his father, I clearly had nothing to say to him as he attempted to explain his reasons for his actions.

Judging by Q's words and demeanor 10 years after we had been acquainted, I was left with the impression that Q struggled with some sort of mental disorder, which would explain a lot, especially if it was hereditary. He seemed stuck in a time warp, back at the place of that 17 year old boy, only now a grown man, aged physically, but not mentally.

Shortly after the incident with Q, I began working at JC Penney. It was nice to be doing something other than sitting around the house while my family made me feel as if *I* was nothing. Plus, I was making money to save and counting down the days until Eric would come back to get me and take me away from my family forever.

One day while leaving work, I ran into Alicia, a friend's older sister, whom I knew from high school in California. I had no idea that she lived in Beaufort, of all places. It turned out that she had married a Marine, and they were stationed in Beaufort. The best news of all was that my friend, Shanelle, who I had not seen or heard from in over a year, had just moved to Beaufort with Alicia and her brother-in-law as well. I was ecstatic!

From that day on, I spent most of my free time at Alicia's with Shanelle. We didn't do much more than hang out at Alicia's house, but it was great just to have friends around. One night, we decided to go to a local club, Studio 7. It was my first time at the club, and I wasn't impressed by the looks of it. What did catch my eye was a group of guys on the dance floor. It was immediately obvious that they were not locals; they were either visiting or were possibly Marines. Either way, they dressed, walked, talked, and danced differently. They were the center of attention, and I, loving to dance, joined right into their group. My friends joined, too, and with no questions asked, the dance floor cleared as we *all* became the center of attention, dancing like a scene straight out of a movie.

The guys were up for a challenge as we moved into their space, but soon after, we all found ourselves paired off with one another. We laughed, joked, and had a blast. It was the most fun I'd had, or should I say *was allowed to have* in years.

One of the guys, Malik, was 21, from Washington, DC, and a Marine stationed in Beaufort. I wasn't attracted to him at first. For one thing, I was engaged and very much in love, committed to Eric, and wasn't looking for anyone else. Even with all of Eric's issues and abuse, I was still loyal to him. Also, Malik, which was his chosen Muslim name – his parents had named him Miguel – struck me as someone I wouldn't otherwise be interested in on any level. Though I had made it clear that I was engaged and not looking to meet or date anyone, he insisted that we could at least be friends if that was all I wanted.

By the end of the night, my friends and I decided to go with the guys for breakfast at Waffle House. One of Malik's friends, O.B., and my friend Shanelle began dating shortly after that night, so we all always hung out together.

Malik proved himself to be just the friend he had said he could be and never pressed me to date him. I believe in platonic friendships between men and women, and I didn't see anything wrong with us being friends. I never tried to hide our friendship because I felt doing so would make it look scandalous. In high school, and even in some cases throughout my adult life, some of my best and most trusting friendships were with men. Though I can't say all of them didn't have any ulterior motives in their friendships with me, they respected me. No, we weren't "friends with benefits" either, just strictly *friends*. Of course my parents didn't understand or believe that was true. From time to time, Malik would help me out by providing a ride to and from work. Some days my parents couldn't, and at times, just *wouldn't* give me rides.

As our friendship grew, I began to talk to Malik about Eric. It was clear to him that I wasn't happy. Eric had become distant and hard to reach. He wasn't answering or returning my phone calls, and when he did call, I was always at work and couldn't talk.

One night he called me at work and was screaming so loudly over the phone, I had no choice but to hang up so that passing customers couldn't hear him. Needless to say, he called back several times, even more irate with each call, until I finally disconnected the phone, afraid of losing my job.

Hanging up on Eric that night is pretty much my last memory of any communication between us. He stopped calling and writing me, and he stopped sending calling cards for me to call him. Yet for months I remained faithful to him, assuming his duties overseas had him preoccupied but that all would be well between us once he returned back to the States.

It wasn't until a month before his return that I was finally able to call and reach him. I was in Baltimore visiting a friend, and I still remember it as if it *just* happened. It was about 1:00 or 2:00 a.m., and I was in the kitchen on the phone. I was connected to his workplace by an overseas operator, and when the line was picked up, I asked to speak to Lance Corporal Lythe.

The voice on the other end sounded agitated and defensive when she asked who I was. Knowing that she was a co-worker, I wasn't bothered by her tone and said that I was his fiancée, then told her my name. At that point, she grudgingly told me that she wasn't going to get him because *she* was his girlfriend, that he no longer loved or wanted me, and for me to never call him again.

My heart began to race faster, pounding in my chest, as my mind tried to comprehend what she was saying. I was naïve, and could only think that it made no sense that his co-worker would speak to me in such a nasty tone, and on top of it all, tell me those terrible things. Shaken, I dismissed her words and asked again to speak to Lance Corporal Lythe, knowing that she wouldn't risk hanging up on me or furthering the conversation on her military work phone.

I heard Eric approaching and yelling at her. Feeling reassured by him putting her in her place, I was confident that he would immediately apologize and explain his crazed co-worker's actions. I waited for him to get on the phone.

Well, when he did, I received a barrage of accusations, excuses, name-calling, and disrespect. He repeated every word his co-worker had just said to me and stated that I no longer needed to call him anymore. He said that he was in a relationship, and that I had just upset his girlfriend by calling him at his job.

After two years of verbal abuse, disrespect, fear, and my faithfulness to a man who clearly wasn't faithful to me, Eric basically ended it all, miles away across the ocean, over the phone, and by cold-heartedly telling me that this woman was there for him when I couldn't be. He told me that she was now pregnant; he was going to get out of the military to marry her, and that this situation was entirely *my* fault. Eric had no remorse for his actions and his tone didn't insinuate the least bit of compassion as he continued to blame me with his irrational accusations. Then he slammed the phone down.

I remember having my back against the wall, phone in hand, and hot tears rolling down my cheeks as I slid to the floor, shaking. I felt so numb inside and out, and the room felt as if it were spinning. I sat there on the floor, filled with mixed emotions, until my friend's mother came into the kitchen to check on me as I burst into uncontrollable tears.

I was in such pain that all she could do was hug me and cry with me. When I could finally piece words together to tell her what had happened, I remember her saying my name repeatedly, empathetically in a soft, motherly voice. You know, when someone is hurting so much that you can't find the right words to console them and all you can say is their name? At least it lets them know that you acknowledge their pain. I remember that because it was the first time anyone had said my name that way, but over the years, I would come to despise it because I didn't want people's pity

After awhile, I pulled myself together somewhat, but I was still sitting on the floor. I called my mother. Hearing her voice as she picked up, tears began to well up inside of me again. Funny how you can fight, rebel, and grow, but still in times of great emotional strain, you want your mother.

"Takiya, what's wrong?" she asked me, waking from her sleep with motherly concern. For a moment I was comforted and let go of inhibitions and the past, needing her so very much to be that loving, compassionate, and understanding mother.

"Mommy, Eric cheated on me," I sobbed to her.

"What?" she asked, her tone switching from concerned to agitation.

"He cheated on me, and the girl is pregnant," I repeated, feeling as if her anxiety was fueled by the fact that this man whom she and my dad had trusted with their daughter could do such a thing.

Unfortunately, I was naïve to have thought that her distress was *for* me and not directed *at* me. My mother spent roughly five minutes on the phone with me, reprimanding me for calling and waking her at such an hour with an issue that she felt wasn't worth talking about at all.

"If he wants to leave, let him leave! What are you crying for, anyway? You don't cry over a man, girl! Don't ever call me and wake me up again for nothing like this."

Looking back on that now, and through more trials over time, I learned to develop a "Never let 'em see you cry" attitude and remember times where I even made it my goal to make a man cry. It made me feel powerful and in control to be able to hurt a man so deeply that he would cry. Unfortunately, I didn't recognize then that true, unconditional love for me could be hidden behind that emotion that I took pride in breaking.

YOUR JOURNAL

Have you ever needed someone to be there for you, only to find that the very person you needed wasn't? What happens when you can't depend or rely on others to assist you in your time of need? Make a list of people, places and things that you feel are needed in your life, and for what reasons.

CHAPTER SEVEN

But I tell you, Love your enemies
and pray for those who persecute you.

– Matthew 5:44

My friend Malik, who eventually became my boyfriend and the father of my first child, was there to help ease the heartache and pain from my transition into life after Eric. In the initial days after the break up, Malik was there to listen, encourage, and advise. As I searched for answers to the "Why's?" he would always insist that I deserved better, that I wasn't the one who was wrong, and that it made him furious knowing that Eric had treated me so badly.

I remember sitting on a bench outside the bowling alley one night, arguing with Malik because I had told him that he didn't care enough about me. He never asked what I was doing, where I was going, or who I was with. My thought processes was so twisted that I correlated jealousy and possessiveness with love. Malik was upset and frustrated that I wanted him to be that way and couldn't understand that *that* wasn't love.

I thought I was really making my point until he snatched the lapels of my coat and pulled me close to him. "Is this what you want?!" he yelled. "For me to treat you like Eric? Because if it is, I can't give you that!"

He scared me speechless, but as quickly as he grabbed me, he let me go, then pulled me into his arms to hug me and to tell me, for the first time, that he loved me. From that point on, I allowed Malik loving me to guide my emotions towards him. I didn't love him back at that point, but I loved spending time with him. We had fun together, and he was different. Secretly, I was still hurting and getting over Eric, so it took time for me to make room in my heart for Malik.

When I was 20 years old, my first child, a beautiful baby girl, whom I named Nikole, was given to me.

It wasn't until I was in the middle of my first pregnancy, and Malik and I had broken up, that I developed any sort of real feelings for him. I look back on the situation as typical "Baby Mama Drama Syndrome." As much as it makes me cringe to put myself in that category, I have to honestly say that I was there.

After the break up with Eric, Malik and I dated for several months before I conceived. We never had any true issues or arguments prior to breaking up; all I recall is that he broke up with me, we remained friends and still communicated, and nothing much changed except the label that defined what we were – or weren't – to one another.

Like most young women, I accepted the shortcomings of giving the proverbial "milk" without the man "buying the cow." This disrespect for myself, as well as my acceptance of verbal abuse, led to my descent into low self-esteem and a misconstrued idea of my own worth. I began to look at sex as a way to communicate love, unspoken desire, and attachment, when it really was nothing more than just plain old sex. I felt like I was in control of a relationship when I gave up the very thing I should have been treasuring the most: my body.

Needless to say, I wasn't truly in control, which was proven as Malik began to date other women after Nikole was born. I felt as if he owed me something, when the truth of the matter was that he didn't owe me anything more than to be a good father to our daughter. But I couldn't understand: we had a child together and still had a physical relationship, yet we weren't a couple. I didn't realize that I was making a decision to allow him to have all the benefits of a committed relationship without the actual commitment.

After awhile, the thought of it all infuriated and changed me. I began to despise Malik. I hated him for throwing me away, just like Eric had. I felt used and deceived, like I wasn't good enough for him. Here I was, dealing with hurt from another man who had claimed to have loved me so dearly yet was hurting me so deeply.

The thing is, though, that I never let Malik know that I was hurting. He would ask what he had done to me to deserve my nasty and spiteful attitude. I had vowed to not let another man have the satisfaction of knowing that he'd hurt me. I honestly think that a lot of the hurt from my relationship with Eric had resurfaced, and that, combined with my anger towards Malik, caused him to experience the wrath of this woman scorned.

I made his life as miserable as I possibly could by starting arguments and calling him at his job, where he wasn't allowed to receive calls except for emergencies. In addition, I made phone calls late at night when I knew a girlfriend was around, or worse, popped up at his home unannounced when a girlfriend was there. Looking back on it now, and though it would have been wrong on his part, I was blessed that Malik never physically abused or snapped on me because I was very belligerent and disrespectful to him, and to the company he kept. There were even times that he let me have my way when it came down to a "me or her" ultimatum. It was stupid, but back then, it didn't matter to me.

My daughter's father was then and still is a good man. I didn't see it then, but I do now, and believe that I hurt and emotionally scarred him so deeply that I can only continue to pray that God heals his heart and mind toward me and allows him to be free of all the things I ever said or did to him in the time of my hurt and anger.

At some point, Malik got tired of my games, my attitude, and my efforts to break up his relationships only to back away from him, just to prove that I could. After awhile, nothing I did seemed to bother him, and even more disturbing, he truly seemed like he couldn't care less about me.

Malik was deployed to Japan when Nikole was about 8 or 9 months old, and when he came back, he was very focused on our baby girl, as any father should be. Overwhelmed at being a young, unwed mother, I continued to add fuel to the fire whenever Malik didn't meet a need or I struggled financially, physically, or emotionally. He loved Nikole, but his life seemed so much easier than mine: he could get up and go, accept or decline watching Nikole, not have to make late trips to the emergency room, and could tell me, "I don't have it," when money was needed. All of this made me even more hostile, and now that he seemed to not care about me, I used the one person he did care about against him: Nikole.

I began to make selfish decisions that controlled when he could and couldn't see her. This seemed to get his attention, and it sparked so much emotional anxiety in his life that he needed therapy, and not of his own free will, but at the clear suggestion of friends, family, and his superiors in the Marine Corps. I turned so cold-hearted and evil toward him that it shames me to think about it, though at the time I wasn't ashamed of it. I was proud of my behavior. I felt empowered and in control. I had been hurt, and I now had the power to hurt. I did and said such hurtful things – like threatening to take Nikole and move away from him – that it would often break him, and he couldn't do anything but cry. I didn't care and wasn't moved by his tears. It brought me a sick satisfaction that allowed me to feel in control.

There wasn't a true release of forgiveness and sincerity between the two of us until ten years later. After I had matured and accepted Christ in my life, Malik told me that he had plotted to kill me during those times. He wasn't joking. But the grace and mercy of God changed Malik's heart. God covered me while satan used me, and I am still here.

Although they had never formally met Malik, my parents had made a judgment from Day One that he was a "no good Marine," and they never truly gave him a chance until my pregnancy. They were always skeptical about Malik's intentions toward me since he already had a son out of wedlock from a previous relationship.

It seemed to me that whatever I wanted in life, my parents tried to see that I had exactly the opposite. When I was in love with and engaged to Eric, they had done everything in their power to keep me from being happy with him. I say "they," but my dad and I were barely on speaking terms. I always knew that most of my mother's hateful words and deeds were fueled by his actions or prompting. I didn't learn until years later, when I reconnected with Eric, that there were times he would call, only to be told that I wasn't there when I actually was. My sister confessed that she was told to say that I wasn't around when he called. After hearing these things, it became a little clearer why he might get so irate and insistent that I was cheating on him or lying about what I did with my time. This is the image my own family was painting of me.

Months after having Nikole, I was living back at my parent's home; before that, I'd moved in with Alicia while her husband was deployed overseas. I remember napping in my room, waiting for Malik to drop off diapers and to visit with Nikole and me. Quite a bit of time had gone by when I was awakened by my sister coming into my room. She had a large gift bag full of diapers and clothes for Nikole. When I asked where Malik was, she told me that he had left already. I asked her why he didn't come in to at least see Nikole or why no one had awakened me. I was shocked and angered to hear her say, "Mommy told me to tell him you were not here."

"Was he upset?" I asked, knowing the answer already, because I had told him I would be home. He was returning from a long road trip from Washington, DC, and he wanted to see his daughter. I stormed down the hall to find my mother sitting in her room. When I reached her, I had not yet calmed down, and angry and crying, I began questioning her. My mother immediately denied that she had done what my sister had said, and even threatened to take me outside in the back yard to fight me for my questioning her and being disrespectful.

As mad as I was, and as confused as I was about why she would keep her grandchild from seeing her father, I went numb when she threatened to fight me. Even with all the hurt, neglect, lies and frustration I had grown up with, it had never once entered my mind to physically attack my mother. She was *my mother*, and even with the offer on the table and scars from the past torn wide open again, that option was still foreign to me. I loved her and just couldn't understand why she seemed to hate me so much.

When I look back on instances where I had fought someone, particularly men, it was because I really wanted to do them harm: make them physically feel the emotional pain they had inflicted on me. I wanted to leave a visible scar on them of the hurt they had caused me. Now here was my very own mother threatening, unfairly, to do the same to me. I remember crying and asking her why she would think I would want to fight her.

"You're my mom," I told her. "I would never try to fight you." Finally my mother, who had gotten up in my face, backed away.

When I did finally talk to Malik, he of course was upset about why he could never seem to come over. He asked me why my mom would do such a thing. Not able to give him a solid answer, I decided to confide in him about my past and the current state of my family's dysfunction. I was nervous that he, too, would call me a liar and question the truth of my statements, but to my surprise, he didn't. He believed me; he trusted my words and consoled me. He never became angry or emotional about the way they had treated me. He showed concern for both Nikole and me, but I promised him that I would never allow anything to happen to Nikole.

Confiding in Malik gave me confidence, and I felt reassured having someone who loved me, believed me, wanted to protect me and to heal the pain. I wanted to prove my words even more, so I suggested that he, my mother, and I sit down to discuss what she had done, as she was still denying that she had told my sister to turn him away when I was home. He agreed.

My mother, on the other hand, refused when I arranged to call and have the three of us on the phone. She simply wouldn't pick up the phone when I asked her to, and angrily told me that she didn't have to prove herself to me or him. She denied even knowing what I was talking about and dismissed me as if I had made the whole incident up. When I brought up the fact that she had involved my sister in her lie, she grew even angrier and threatened to "kick my butt" yet again. That was the end of that discussion.

Sometime later, Malik suggested to me that he talk privately with my mom to see if there was anything he could do to soften her or my dad toward him. Not totally comfortable with the idea, because I knew she would be angry with me, I reluctantly agreed. Some way, somehow, my mom agreed to talk with Malik, and I remember the day just as clearly as if it were yesterday.

I was home, and Malik asked if I would go inside to allow him a chance to talk to my mother on the porch. My stepfather, at this point, was overseas in Italy. Unbeknownst to my mother and Malik, I snuck into my sister's room – she was away at school – lifted her window pane, which faced the porch, and listened to their entire conversation.

Malik wanted to know why my parents had never gotten to know him or given him a chance to come around and be welcomed. He talked about himself and the things he wanted for Nikole and said that he had no bad intentions toward either of us.

My mother quickly blamed me. She claimed that I had never spoken of Malik and was cheating on Eric with him, which they disapproved of. Of course, since I'd called her on the night I found out Eric had cheated on me, my mother knew that Eric was no longer a part of my life. She told Malik that I was a liar and not to be trusted, even claiming that what I had told her about my dad touching me – something I had just shared with Malik – was just a lie to get attention.

At this point, I had heard enough. I was fuming and stormed out of the house and onto the porch to confront my mother, only to have Malik tell me to calm down and go back inside. Neither of them seemed to want me involved in a conversation *about me*. That day was the last day that I considered Malik to be my friend, because he believed every word my mother told him. Maybe because my mother was older, Malik couldn't possibly fathom her lying about these things. For some time, my parents had a better relationship with Malik than Nikole and I did, and they communicated more with each other than Nikole and I did with any of them.

YOUR JOURNAL

One of the worst feelings is when you are characterized as a liar but are telling the truth, especially when it comes to matters of character and integrity. Though we would much rather speak up and speak out to be heard, the Bible tells us to pray for those who lie, persecute, and despise us. Take this time to write out a sincere prayer for the person or people who have harmed you or done you wrong.

CHAPTER EIGHT

But when He, the Spirit of Truth, comes, He will guide you into all the Truth. For He will not speak His own message; but He will tell whatever He hears; He will give the message that has been given, and He will announce and declare to you the things that are to come.

– John 16:13

While my dad was away in Italy, he and my mom would communicate with one another constantly by email. One day in particular, I recall sitting down to use the computer and noticed my name in an email. My mother had apparently forgotten to log out of her account, let alone close the email she had been reading; it was still open and in plain view on the screen. It was from my stepdad, and though I had no intention of reading her private mail, my curiosity at seeing my name prompted me to read on. What I read made my heart pound in my ears, and my eyes stung as tears of anger welled up and rolled down my cheeks.

My dad had written a barrage of attacking words, calling me "lazy," a "whore," a "slut," and every other foul, degrading word that no woman, let alone your own daughter, should be called. He said I was an "unfit mother," "stupid," "dumb," and "evil," and talked about me as if I were worthless. The email was sprinkled with jokes about how I would never amount to anything more than a recipient of the public housing assistance I had just been approved for.

Reading further, I could see email after email between them as they took turns degrading me, putting me down, and questioning my morals, motherhood, and very existence, it seemed to me.

My mother complained of having to drive me around for WIC, doctor's appointments, and shopping, and even referring to me by using the same names that my dad had, never once defending me, or seeming to show disapproval of his constant attacks on me. Honestly, I can't imagine why my mother, or any mother at all, would treat her own child, especially one undeserving of such name-calling, as she did.

I couldn't understand it, nor could I believe it. What was even more disturbing was that all of their conversations seemed to consist of was attacking me. Most of it was lies, or when it was the truth, it was twisted and stretched beyond recognition. There were pages and pages, email after email. All I could think was that they both hated me. I was both furious and wounded beyond compare. I wanted to hurt them both at that point and even thought about burning our house down.

I printed the emails – at least 20 pages of them – and went to my bedroom, shut and locked the door, and began highlighting everything that referred to me. I was going to confront my mother and wanted proof to show Malik, whom they also mentioned negatively. I wanted proof of those words and statements to throw back in my mother's face. I felt these emails were justification to scream, cuss, and blow up at her. This time, I felt that if she wanted to fight, I was going to oblige her and go in it fueled by all the hurtful, disgusting lies they had told about me. What mother allows – let alone participates in – saying such hateful things about her child?

Looking back, I can see and appreciate where God's mercy and voice began to change my life and heart. I never did confront my mother that day, nor to this day have I discussed the content of those emails with her, my dad, or anyone else, actually. I held on to those printed pages for months, waiting to use them as ammunition, yet as time went on, I learned that revenge wasn't what satisfied me. God was about to start showing me His way: a better way of doing things.

In December 1997, two weeks before Nikole was born, I had been invited to a local church by Carrie, my boss. She was the owner of a local pre-school, and from the moment I had met her, she was kind and compassionate to me. She took a genuine interest in my well-being, as I was eight months pregnant when she hired me, and even then she saw potential in me, something that I never knew I had and wouldn't recognize until I was well into my early 30s. She lived by the words of her preschool's mission, from Ephesians 4:32: "And be ye kind one to another, tenderhearted, forgiving one another, even as God for Christ's sake hath forgiven you." She was the first person in my life in a long time who seemed to really care about me. So when she invited me to church, saying yes and going was easy.

I didn't know much about church principles, etiquette in church, or even Jesus, but when the invitation was made to come to the altar to accept Jesus as my Lord and Savior, I knew it was right and what I wanted to do. I can't even begin to explain it as anything but God's guiding hand in my life; within myself, I just knew.

On Sunday, December 14, 1997, at 1:24 pm, I received salvation and was led to the Lord, just days before the birth of my baby girl.

Months later, I sat reading the Bible and learning to pray and listen for God's voice. I battled within about how to handle the horrible emails: should I keep them? Hold on to them and use them to my advantage, to show everyone what my family thought of me and how they treated me? That was what *my own reasoning* was telling me to do: "Hurt them and make them pay" raced around my mind, but in my heart, deep in my soul, I softly heard "Throw the emails away and never speak of them. Forgive them and pray for them."

At the time, I didn't know that inner voice was the Spirit of God speaking to me, but I knew how God felt about forgiveness and righteousness. I knew that it would be pleasing to Him if I let it go. Honestly, it took a few days before I brought myself to shred every piece of those emails, but I did, as I allowed God to begin mending, healing, and filling my heart towards my family.

When Nikole was about six months old, we moved out of my parents' house into a place of our own. It was the first of anything that was my very own. It was a modestly sized, one bedroom apartment in Yemassee, South Carolina, a town even smaller than Beaufort, about 30 minutes away. I had recently purchased my first car, a 1989 Honda Civic. I was working full-time at the pre-school, which Nikole was able to attend as well, and I even saved money, thanks to my employee discount for child care.

I considered Carrie, the pre-school's owner, to be family: she and her husband were now Nikole's godparents. Carrie gave me my first Bible: a white leather-bound King James Version that I kept for years before passing it on as a gift to a close friend and newfound Christian. I loved reading the Bible and kept it with me all the time. Whenever I was able to find a moment of solitude, I would sit in my car and read.

At this point in my life, I was reflecting and writing, and my receiving salvation and allowing Jesus in offered immediate results in my life. I was at peace, happy, and seemed to have some direction in my life. I didn't find this out until years later, but apparently other employees noticed my devotional time and referred to me as "the saved girl." They didn't know my name, but they knew that I was a Christian, and to me that was something worth being proud of.

One of my favorite songs of worship was and still is Juanita Bynum's "Peace." The lyrics of the song referred to God being our peace regardless of everything going on in our lives. The melody was soft and calming as the singer repeated, "You are my peace. You are my peace, and I worship you. Peace. Peace. Peace." I played it endlessly throughout the day as the children played and napped as well as in the car and at home. Back then, learning and growing as a Christian, I had not been introduced to the knowledge and power of the spirit that is in music, but I can see how my life, spirit, and soul were in sync with that song. God was preparing me a foundation to strengthen and establish me amidst turmoil and strife in my life.

After so many tumultuous years, and now at this place of such peace, I had no idea of the many years of trials, anguish, and pain that were to come. But God knew, and He set me up with one of most powerful spiritual tools a Christian will ever need, which is the gift and ability to hear Him speak.

One morning, while getting ready for church, I was overpowered by a sudden urgent need to call my mom. When she answered she sounded groggy, but there was something else in her voice. "Mommy, what's wrong?" I asked.

She tried to keep her composure, but by the end of her sentence, her voice cracked with tension, and the strain turned into sobs as she let me know that my dad was in a coma.

"What?" I exhaled, shocked. My dad was still overseas in Italy, and it was winter. He had been leading troops over some icy railroad tracks when he slipped, fell, and hit his head on the tracks. Fear crept up my body, but I remained calm for my mother, as I asked her more detailed questions. He had already been in the hospital for two days prior to them calling my mother, and he was showing no signs of response or recovery. Listening to my mother sound so upset, helpless, and fearful, I knew that I would do and say anything that I could to console her and show her compassion.

I immediately regained my composure and pushed away my negative thoughts and fear and calmly prayed with my mother. I let her know that I was going to church, where they would pray for my father, and that I would come over after service. I told her that he would be okay, and for the first time ever in my life, I knew that God would answer my prayers. I felt so calm and so sure that I even surprised myself by choosing to continue on to church instead of rushing over to my parents' house.

At church, I gave a message to Carrie to have my dad added to the prayer list, and she immediately got the message to the pastor. During service, he called for the entire congregation to begin praying for my dad. This day was the first day ever that I truly realized what it felt like to let go of a situation and really let God handle it. Through all the awful, hurtful, demeaning, and disappointing encounters with my family and our past, particularly my father, I didn't have it in my heart to find any comfort in knowing that he was dying. I felt the heart-wrenching fear and my mother's tears as I visualized her life without my dad. My sister was still in high school, and I was barely established; we were just too young to even comprehend taking care of my mother and filling a gap that would be left should he die. I, personally, wasn't ready to take on that responsibility.

I shouted, praised, worshiped, screamed, cried, and rejoiced for God healing my dad and waking him from that coma. I yelled at the devil like he was standing in front of me and commanded him to take his hand off my dad. I was God's child, and He would answer those prayers for me, and I knew it.

A couple of hours later, I confidently headed to my parents' house to check on my mom. She was now out of bed, eyes bloodshot and puffy from crying, but she offered good news: During service, she had received a phone call from the hospital letting her know that my dad had come out of the coma and was now up.

YOUR JOURNAL

Can you imagine placing yourself in the position of one who has been so hurt, put down and mistreated for so long, then suddenly having the tables turned: Those who hurt you are now needing and calling on you. Write about what you would do, then what you feel God would have you do.

CHAPTER NINE

Behold! I have given you authority and power to trample upon serpents and scorpions,
and physical and mental strength and ability over all the power that the enemy possesses; and nothing shall in any way harm you.
– Luke 10:19

After my dad returned from Italy, things seemed to take a turn for the better in my family's relationships with each other. We were not quite what a family should be, but my dad's near-death experience had given us all a sense of appreciation and love for one another. Beyond Vacation Bible School, we had never attended church as a family during my childhood. However, after the accident and my dad's return to the States, my parents visited my church a couple of times.

The hurt and sting of the past was nowhere close to being erased from my memory, but as I continued my growth as a Christian – going to church, reading the Bible, and seeking counsel from other friends and members of the congregation – I began to forgive. Forgiveness, for me, has always come more easily than most people think it ought to. The key to my being able to forgive was that I always pushed bad incidents to the far recesses of my mind. Perhaps it was instilled in me from childhood; growing up and having situations ignored could have taught me to harbor them in forgetfulness. As the rest of my family went on with life as if nothing had happened, *I* was forced to move on with life as if nothing happened. Strange as it may sound, I found myself carrying that trait well on into my adulthood. Forgiveness simply came from forgetting. And perhaps forgetting came from not wanting to deal with situations. Maybe I was running from my fears.

In 1998, when my daughter was about two years old, I had my first experience, or should I say "run in," with the law. I was working as a preschool teacher, and at some point during my employment, Malik's ex-girlfriend, Leslie, started working at the same place. We never had any issues with one another, and though our children shared the same father, we were pretty cordial. Our co-workers and my mother felt that it didn't make sense for us to befriend one another. Our casual friendliness initiated my first episode of a spiral into temporary madness.

At this point, Malik and I were not involved in a committed relationship, but we still had sex from time to time. A co-worker, Melissa, consistently spread gossip and antagonized me about my developing friendship with Leslie. Several times she insinuated that Malik was being unfaithful to us both by continuing to have sexual relationships with both of us. Melissa suggested that Leslie was only pretending that she liked me to get information about Malik and me.

I believed her, and felt betrayed, made a fool of, and scared. I became so upset one day at all the gossip and hurtful words that I ended up leaving work early. Melissa had moved on from speaking solely to me about her thoughts to spreading rumors throughout the entire daycare facility to co-workers and parents.

I learned of the on-going gossip from Carrie, who pulled me out of class one day to ask me what was going on. Carrie questioned me to clarify the matter, which only infuriated me. I felt ashamed and put on the spot by all of Melissa's heckling and derogatory words about how stupid I was being.

I packed up my things and my daughter and headed straight to Malik's house. When I arrived, I found Malik just getting home from a long, frustrating day himself, and apparently he was in no mood to discuss the past or present day gossip and drama. I angrily questioned him about whether he was still sleeping with both Leslie and me. He only stared at me, refusing to answer. His silence kindled my anger. I don't even remember putting Nikole down or letting her out of my sight, but I know I followed Malik into his bedroom, picked up his glasses, and snapped them in half to get his attention.

From that point on, I turned into a tornado of destruction, picking up anything of value – sentimental or financial – and destroying it. I wanted him to hurt the way that I was hurting, and the more I thought about my humiliation at work, the deeper I raged.

I have no recollection of where Malik and Nikole were during my destructive spree, but I literally went from one end of his house to the other, breaking glass, shattering mirrors, knocking over things and tearing up property. I was so enraged that I felt as if I couldn't stop myself, as if there was a driving force fueling my anger and directly controlling my thoughts and actions.

The last thing I remember breaking were two solid stainless steel swords that Malik had received as a gift for his deployment in Japan. I grabbed the largest and used it to bash and wreck anything still standing, including a glass and metal coffee table in the center of the living room. I swung the steel sword so forcefully against the metal that the sword actually broke into two pieces.

I don't know if Malik put me out or if I left, but I ended up outside, kicking and banging on his car. My rage grew even greater, fueled by Malik holding Nikole and refusing to give her to me. I screamed and yelled and kicked and punched him, but he wouldn't let her go.

At some point, he had called the police, and I could hear the sirens in the distance. I jumped in my car, intending to leave, and threw it in reverse, but as clearly as if someone were sitting next to me, I heard the words, "Run him over."

Without a second thought, I threw my car into Drive and floored the gas, aiming directly at Malik. In my state of rage, I had forgotten he was holding Nikole. I looked right into my daughter's tearful eyes as she screamed. I slammed on my brakes.

The next thing I recall is guns pointing at me, voices yelling at me, angry faces, and rough hands pulling me out of my car, slamming me on the cold concrete driveway, and tightening handcuffs on my wrists. In a state of shock as I sat in the back of the police car, the reality of what I had done came flooding back as I looked at Malik, now crying and trying to comfort our sobbing, shaking daughter.

I began to shake, too, crying hysterically, not knowing what was to come. I had only seen people go to jail on TV and in movies. Was I going away forever? Was Malik going to tell them to lock me up for good?

That night, I sat numbly in a cold cement room, tearfully trying to figure out all that had happened. I had been brought in, booked, searched, and photographed. I was told that in the morning, I would see the judge who would determine whether I would be released or not.

The next morning as I entered the judge's chambers, I was surprised to see Malik and to hear him state that he didn't want to press charges, nor did he want to see me locked up. We never spoke directly but exchanged glances of mutual hurt and confusion. I was released with a pending court date; though he'd refused to press charges, the county would proceed against me because of the 911 call and what police had witnessed at the scene.

I was charged with criminal domestic violence and malicious injury to personal property and ordered to attend General Sessions Court weekly until my trial date. Basically, when you are facing a criminal charge, if you are not locked up from Day One, you are required to report for a roll call of sorts as proof that you have not fled the area and intend to appear at the time of your trial. One missed appearance would result in being locked up until trial and receiving further charges.

By God's grace, I wasn't charged with attempted murder for trying to run Malik over. I was assigned a public defender because I couldn't afford an attorney, and for months I anxiously awaited my final trial.

Within six months, I was released from having to attend General Sessions and, thanks to my attorney's diligent efforts, my charges were dropped and expunged from my record: completely removed as if nothing had ever happened.

This was testimony and proof of God's hand in my life; it typically takes years and a lot of money for criminal reports to be removed from a record. I didn't have to pay a dime, but the damage to Malik, to our relationship, and to my parental duties would linger for many years. I didn't know it then, but this was only the first of the overnight stays that I would have at the Beaufort County Detention Center, all resulting from abusive or violent relationships, both on my part and that of men I was involved with.

YOUR JOURNAL

Snickering whispers and judgmental stares can be enough to make just about anyone want to speak up in self-defense. Even more, the sting of hurtful gossip can be enough to drive you over the edge. Yet, as God's Word says, He has given us mental and physical strength over our enemies' power to control us. Recognizing the enemy's device of control will enable you to begin to defeat evil, time and time again. Write about your traits and characteristics that emerge as a signal that the enemy is attempting to control you.

CHAPTER TEN

For if you return to the Lord, your brethren and your children shall find compassion with their captors and return to this land.
For the Lord your God is gracious and merciful,
and He will not turn away His face from you if you return to Him.

– 2 Chronicles 30:9

I was about 23 when I met Scott, a man 11 years my senior, in a local nightclub. I had no sense of what a real man was or how a godly man would carry himself, so receiving a rose from a random man whose eye I had caught was acceptable enough. It was Valentine's weekend, and my friends and I were out clubbing, which had become our routine on Friday and Saturday nights.

I can still clearly recall the way he watched my every move from across the room, like a lion hunting its prey. Scott was charming, good-looking, and seemed sincere in his interest toward me. We dated for a couple of months before his true personality began to show. He was possessive, demanding, and openly unfaithful. He made it clear that he could and would come and go as he pleased; however, I was to be available at his beckoning call.

Initially, Scott never spoke derogatorily to me, and I don't really ever recall us arguing, but he controlled me because he was older, paid the bills, and made me feel as if I was "chosen" and privileged to have caught his eye. If I didn't like how he acted, he would have no problem leaving.

With my low self-esteem and no standards, I continuously accepted his terms by staying with him. I could never prove that Scott was unfaithful because he never allowed me to overstep certain boundaries, until one day I found him talking to my neighbor at her window. I had already told him that I thought she was going after him, and though he had dismissed my accusations, I could see the spark of interest in his eye.

Agitated, I began questioning him, which was something I had never done before, and he apparently believed this was something I should never do. He raised his voice and ordered me to go back inside. We exchanged words, yelling and cussing at one another, with him showing no regard for me in front of my neighbor as he called me "stupid," "ignorant," "dumb," and "pathetic."

The lack of respect and a lifetime of familiarity with being called those words enraged me. Tiring of the scene and defeated because I just wasn't going to shut up, Scott got in his car to leave. Still wanting to argue and prove to him that I didn't have to take how he was treating me, I got in my car and followed him, just as he had done to me on so many occasions. He lived less than five minutes away, and when he made it home, he locked the door behind him but continued to yell profanities and insults from the window of his second floor apartment.

I became so enraged that I pulled and kicked at his front door until I damaged it. My actions, and the scene arising, angered Scott. He didn't like the fact that we were now at his home making a scene, and he came outside, pushing and shoving me, telling me to leave. As I started to go, he shoved me so forcefully that my initial instinct was to fight back. I ran at him, balled up my fist, and punched him in the face as hard as I could.

Not realizing the repercussions of my actions, I stepped back and began to apologize to him. By this time, a few neighbors, mostly male friends of his, had gathered outside and were laughing at the fact that I had just punched him in front of everyone.

As I watched his face change from shock to rage, Scott grabbed me, pushed me down, then picked me back up off the ground, and punched me back in *my* face. My nose gushed, and as the taste of my blood filled my mouth, I grabbed my face and pulled away as Scott began apologizing.

I got in my car, drove away, and as quickly as the fight had begun, it was over. Never in my life had I been hit by a man. This day will be symbolized for the rest of my life by the bruise that remained on my nose from the ring he was wearing when he hit me. I am constantly reminded of that day when I look in the mirror.

Back at home, as I began to clean up, there was a knock at the door. Scott was fearful that I would call the police, so he had called them first. With correlating stories and the fact that we both hit one another, for the second time within a year, I was handcuffed and taken to jail for domestic violence. I had to spend two hours with a couple of officers who questioned and photographed me. I was then assigned to a victim's advocate officer, given information about women in abusive relationships, and then released.

Scott was also arrested that day and spent the night in jail. After his release and for months after, he tried to communicate with me and apologize, but I'd had enough. At least I knew better than to stay with a man who would hit me.

As is characteristic of most controlling, possessive individuals, Scott didn't take rejection well. I ignored his initial attempts to appear kind and concerned, so he quickly turned malicious. I would often run into him at the local nightclub, and he would do everything in his power to make sure I saw him come or go with one woman after another.

At this point, I had moved on and couldn't have cared less, so my indifference to his actions, coupled with my blatant flirting with and attention from other men, only fueled his fire. Scott slashed my vehicle's tires twice, and would follow me home or to my friends' homes, where he would sit in his car and call me, threatening me for "giving away" what he claimed to be his, because he assumed that I was sleeping around.

One night at the club, he even offered to pay another girl to cut my face with a razor. I didn't know her, nor did she know me, but through God's grace and her compassion, she had refused and actually came to tell me what he wanted her to do to me. She told me to leave before he found someone ignorant enough to do it, and realizing how serious he was, I disappeared from the nightclub scene for quite awhile, staying alert in my everyday surroundings so as not to be caught off-guard. For a bit longer, the nasty, threatening calls or messages came, but eventually they stopped.

Feeling scared and vulnerable, I retreated to my spirituality and relationship with Christ and began to focus more on attending church and living according to the way I felt God wanted me to. I repented for the sins I had allowed myself to get into and for the state of life and relationships I had chosen to live in.

In the summer of 1999, I left my position as a preschool teacher and was hired as a legal assistant. I had no prior experience in the legal field, let alone any administrative experience, yet my knowledge of computers, ability to type, and motivation were the first indications that God had placed an entrepreneurial mindset within me. I quickly and easily moved from one high-paying career to another, back and forth between the legal and medical fields. God had given me grace, favor, wisdom, and knowledge that only He could. Time and again, I was selected for any position I applied for. I worked as a legal assistant, a medical assistant, a retail manager, and an executive administrator for a financial wealth firm – none of which I had gone to school for, or had a degree to qualify me for. I had barely graduated high school due to my rebellious attitude and lack of attendance throughout my senior year.

What I did have was the gift of communication. God blessed me with a mouth to talk, and I knew how to use it. I didn't know it then, but I was also blessed with a talent to write and express myself. I had grown up around diversity and was comfortable in unfamiliar and high-pressure surroundings. I'm not saying I always like it, but some of us just work best that way. God allowed me to retain knowledge, and I caught on to things faster than they could be taught. I only needed to be shown how to do something once before I could do it myself. I was a self-starter, multi-tasker, and initiative-taker, always working on behalf of my employers' best interest.

In early 2000, I was working for a physician as his head assistant. I was content, making as much money as I had asked for, and driving a brand-new company car, one personally picked out for me. Little did I know, in just a few months, God would open new doors and place me on a path to being a business owner myself. I was just 23 years old.

In August of 2000, when Nikole was about two and a half years old, I was still working as a medical assistant, but there were tense days when I couldn't make it to work because she was sick. Though infrequent, my absences were noticeable and affected the physician's schedule. Not having me around to prepare paperwork, screen patients, and write or call in prescriptions was a burden to my boss, and he wasn't happy about it.

The final straw came while he and his wife were on vacation and left me in charge of the practice. Nikole was ill during this time, and since I was only at work to answer phones, I contacted my boss for permission to bring her to work with me. He approved, and I went about the day as usual, closing up at five and heading home. I placed Nikole in the back seat, buckled her in, and quietly drove the 20 minutes home.

Assuming that Nikole had fallen asleep, I never bothered to glance back in the rearview mirror or speak up to check on her. As I pulled into the driveway and shut off the car, I finally turned around to find my daughter straining for air, unable to move because the seat belt, which I had placed across her lap and behind her back, was wrapped around her neck. Shocked, I climbed into the back seat to release and loosen the seat belt, only to panic as I realized that the seat belt had a glitch and would only retract instead of releasing as I pulled.

Unable to breathe and frightened, Nikole began to cry as the seat belt dug into her neck. I slid my fingers between the belt and her neck as much as I could to give her room to breathe, but with her squirming and pulling, it only tightened more and more. I leaned forward, grabbed my cell phone, and without thought, called Scott. Hearing my panic, he began shouting, asking what was wrong and where I was. I dropped the phone, and it rolled out of my reach. I began sobbing and praying for God to please help us as I watched my baby being strangled.

Through my prayers, God calmed me, and I began to think of ways to get her out. If I could just run in the house and grab the scissors, I could cut the belt, but how long would it take me to get them and come back? Would she be okay? I didn't want to take that chance.

I didn't know what to do. We were all alone where we lived: there were only three occupied houses on our isolated road, which was off the main road, and none of my neighbors were home. There was no way that someone passing by would see us.

Though I felt hopeless and defeated, I kept praying. I noticed a car creeping slowly down the pathway, between the trees. It seemed as if the driver was going to pass my house, but it stopped right in front of my driveway. I couldn't get out because my hand was holding the belt off Nikole's neck and any movement could further retract the belt. I eased my body towards the front seat, lifted my foot, and began to kick the horn like a mad woman. The driver had placed his car in park and was just sitting there for what seemed like forever. When he finally got out to see what was going on, I screamed for him to help me. He walked slowly, looking confused, but as he neared my car and could see the situation, he quickly jumped into action, asking what to do. I told him to grab my keys, go into my house, and find the scissors.

He moved as quickly as he could, walking with the type of limp common to those with multiple sclerosis. At this point, Nikole was hoarse from straining to breathe in between cries, and her eyes were heavy from exhaustion.

Our rescuer hurried back and handed me the scissors. I quickly cut Nikole free and embraced my daughter as if for the very first time. Through the tears, I praised and thanked God, then thanked my rescuer, who explained that he didn't know why he had turned down my road, which is why he was driving so slowly. He said he didn't know anyone who lived there and had not even known the road existed until this particular night. Until he had heard my horn, he had just sat in his car with no clue why he was there! But God knew!

My rescuer and I never exchanged names, and our paths have yet to cross again. All I know is that he drove a cream-colored Infinity, and walked with a limp. In his confusion, God had sent him to be at the right place at the right time! Hallelujah!

YOUR JOURNAL

For every action, there is a reaction, and to every reaction, there must be a consequence. In the Bible, this is referred to as "seedtime and harvest." Daily, we are planting some sort of "seed," whether it be in word, deed, or action. These seeds can be positive or negative; however, they will all yield a harvest. We may fail to realize that our harvest can affect more than just ourselves, but our loved ones as well. Take this time to reflect on choices and decisions you have made that have affected others.

CHAPTER ELEVEN

For it is written, He will give His angels charge over you to guard and watch over you closely and carefully.

– Luke 4:10

Just a few short days later, the physician I worked for fired me because I'd missed too much work due to having inadequate child care. Not sure if I would be able to find another position with the same perks and pay as I'd had at that job, and really tired of the drama and issues I was having in Beaufort, I decided to move to St. Louis, Missouri, where all my family now lived.

A year before, my dad had retired from the Marine Corps, and he and my mother had decided to move back to St. Louis, where they had both been born and raised. My sister was now in her freshman year of college at Clemson University in South Carolina. Though I knew that I didn't want to ultimately live with them, I figured that my parents' home, surrounded by all my extended family – my grandmother, aunts, uncles, and cousins – would be a good starting point for a new life.

My house was pretty much packed, and I was about a week away from leaving when I took my daughter to visit her godparents. Her godmother, Carrie, and I discussed other options that would allow me to stay in Beaufort. Her housekeeper was there cleaning, and I remember Carrie asking me what else I thought I could do well.

"Cleaning," I joked, as I watched the maid move from here to there. "It's the reason my mother had kids. If we don't know how to do anything else, we can clean a house. Plus, my dad was a Marine. We had field day at home."

Though I giggled, Carrie intensely pondered what I'd said. "So why can't you clean?" she asked. My smirk dropped as her question sank into my mind, and it took all of 25 seconds for me to grab hold of it. We went into her office, sat at her desk, and began comparing the price of the housekeeping service she was using to what competitive rates I should use. We factored in what supplies I would need, how much time it would take, and where I would need to advertise. We picked a name that would represent perfection every time it was spoken, and "Top Quality Cleaning Service" was begun.

I spent the following day driving through affluent neighborhoods, passing out flyers to advertise the business. I vividly remember my daughter, not quite three years old, standing in the front passenger seat, leaning out the window, placing flyers in mail boxes as I slowly crept along from house to house. She had the biggest smile and felt so important to be involved in Mommy's new business.

That Sunday, we attended church, and after service, I had a message from a physician's wife requesting housekeeping services. My first client! I called her back, went over the rates and services, and booked her for Monday morning. Within three days, the business was born.

For the first year, it was a small operation; I worked alone, serving only residential customers, but after the first year, I hired my first employee and added commercial services.

I was only 23 when God blessed me with the wisdom and the knowledge to operate my first business. Top Quality Cleaning Service grew and flourished for three years until I closed its doors and eventually moved to St. Louis in 2003.

As much as God was blessing me, I had not yet learned what it was to totally love and be faithful to Him. Looking back now, I didn't lack faith, but the area that the devil challenged me in was relationships, whether they were platonic friendships or romantic. I never *needed* a man, but I did have the *desire* for a man. The devil knew that if he could put a man in front of me who had a good personality, made me smile, and promised to show me the world if I was his, I would buy it hook, line and sinker.

I still found it so difficult to meet honest and trustworthy people. They were few and far between; meanwhile, I couldn't seem to stop crossing paths with evil, deceitful, and malicious individuals. I was always a bit too trusting of people I really didn't know and far too naïve when it came to men.

For example, at one time I'd had a platonic so-called friend, Nick, who was supposed to help me move my things from one house to another, only to find that he was actually casing my place and taking inventory of the equipment and items he was coming back to steal from me. He seemed so caring and protective as he walked through my new house, making sure all windows and doors were securely locked to ensure that "no one breaks in" while I slept at my old house and finished packing.

Unbeknownst to me, Nick had left a bathroom window at the rear of the house unlocked so that he could come back later that night to rob me. The next day, while filing a police report, he actually had the audacity to stare in my face and play "concerned friend" as I wept in his arms. It was only months later, while hanging out with friends, that I ran into Nick's girlfriend, who was wearing a brand new matching Coach designer hat and handbag set: the exact set that had been reported stolen from my home. She explained to me that Nick had given them to her as a gift.

Then there was Jeremiah, a big, burly bear of a man, at least 10 years my senior, and only satan knows why I gave this man the time of day. He was overweight, unattractive, and recently released from prison. All he ever did was lie to me about his children, his woman, his fictitious business, and his money. Not only was he a well-versed liar, but he was a thief and a criminal mastermind, all in front of my blind eyes.

His lies started to become clear to me when he stole $800 of my rent money. My landlord had given me notice, and I had struggled to earn enough to pay my past due rent. Jeremiah knew this because I had asked him if I could borrow the money, but, like always, he never had any. At the end of the day, overworked and exhausted, I waited for my landlord to come home, so I could give her the cash. Jeremiah had come over and kept insisting that we go to the movies or out to dinner. I told him I didn't want to leave before giving the landlord her money, but he insisted we should just go, and I could see her when I got back.

"Just keep the money on you," I remember him saying. "It's safer that way."

In the theater parking lot, Jeremiah suggested I should put the money in a bag hidden in the trunk "because no one could get into that." I personally hit the auto locks, slammed my car door shut, and pulled on the handle to double-check. I asked him if his side was locked, and he said it was.

Jeremiah left the movie several times, claiming he had to make a call, needed a drink, or was going to the bathroom. As we headed back to my car, Jeremiah was the first to notice that the driver's side door was slightly ajar. Panic set in; I already knew that I wouldn't find what I was looking for when we searched the vehicle. Just as had happened before, my enemy was the one holding and consoling me as I cried. He even searched the car harder than me and pretended to be angry about it being my rent money as we gave our stories and filed a report with the police.

Alarm bells *finally* started to go off in my head when the officer questioned Jeremiah about entering and exiting the theater, then made a snide statement to Jeremiah about knowing who he was and "the type of person" he was from previous run-ins with the law.

Jeremiah was arrested that night for larceny, and whether I had chosen to press charges or not, he was found guilty in criminal court. I had pressed charges, so he was ordered to pay the amount he'd stolen from me plus an $800 assessment to the court. He paid the court, but as for *my* $800, the court clerk told me that his stealing from me was also a civil matter. I would have to pay to file a civil complaint, then take him to civil court to get my money. I was so frustrated, and without the money to pay to take him to court, I failed to follow through.

Obviously, all communication and contact with Jeremiah stopped, but just as with previous bad men in my life, the devil didn't allow him to just disappear easily. There were times when he would pass me on the road, pointing and clicking his fingers, forming a gun as if to shoot at me. Just as with Scott, I was even told to leave a friend's house – by Scott, of all people, who'd once offered to pay a girl to cut me! – because Jeremiah was sending a few girls over to fight me.

Later that summer, I was contacted by a detective who wanted to ask me questions about my money being stolen. It turned out that Jeremiah was involved in a tri-state counterfeit ring, and the detective really wanted to know if I'd had any involvement with him or information about him. I had never known anything about him dealing in or handling counterfeit money, I told the detective. For the most part, any time he had or spent money, I thought it was drug money, but even then I had never questioned him about it.

It must have been God's grace and protection that kept Jeremiah from ever giving me any money or spending large amounts of it on me. He rarely seemed to even have any money when we were together. I offered the detective what little knowledge I had and later found out that Jeremiah was eventually sent to prison for his involvement in the counterfeit ring. Again, I thank God for never having any involvement or knowledge of his dealings, as there were others, including friends and one of his children's mothers, who were associated with his illegal actions and arrested.

While most of my relationships with men were brotherly friendships, the ease with which I trusted them involved me in more hurtful, dangerous, and even life-threatening situations.

Devon was a friend of a friend whom I had met casually and didn't know well. I had seen him from time to time on the street, at the store, or at the local nightclub. I was never interested in him or attracted to him, but he always seemed to remember me. He was the quiet, soft-spoken type, with a very dark complexion and eyes that had a strange sparkle and glassiness to them. I later realized the glassiness was because he was always high on something, but I can't even really describe the "sparkle." I know now, though, that his grayish green eyes glittered with deception.

For years we remained passers-by, making small talk when we crossed paths, so it *seemed* as if we knew one another. Driving home one day, I passed Devon walking and offered him a ride to his destination, which was near my home. He asked if I wanted to hang out, and since I had no plans, we ended up at my house watching movies. When Devon decided to go hang with friends, we called it a night, he called a friend for a ride, and he left.

Though I had not felt uncomfortable while he was at my house, I felt uneasy when he left. I was suddenly afraid and paranoid about having allowed him to know where I lived. Even though he had said he was going out with friends, for some reason, I began to believe they might come back with him to my place. I peered through my blinds as he left and watched as he stood in my front yard talking to his friend and looking hesitantly at my house before finally getting in the car to leave. I was beginning to feel lightheaded, my paranoia increasing, and my vision getting hazy. It was already pretty late, so I lay down on the couch, hoping to fall asleep and wake up feeling better.

I don't know how much time passed, but when I woke up, I felt worse. I was sweating and so light-headed that every movement felt surreal, as if it were not really happening. My heart was pounding loudly, and my breathing was heavy and raspy. I couldn't make any sense of what was going on, but as clearly as if someone were sitting in the room with me, I heard the voice of God say to me, "Push the couch in the front of the door."

My whole body felt numb, and I could barely move as I struggled to my feet. I hardly had any strength, but I pushed and pushed until finally my couch blocked the door. I then collapsed back onto it and lay there, totally paralyzed, unable to move and thinking that I was dying.

I then noticed the handle at my front door turning, first slowly, then sharply and rapidly. Whoever it was had a key to get in because I was positive that I had locked the door after Devon had left. I watched in fear as the door began to shake as the person on the other side attempted to push it open. I wanted to move, to get up and run, but I couldn't. All I was able to do was lie there in my drugged stupor and wait for what was coming. The struggle with the door didn't last long. The attempt seemed half-hearted or maybe aborted due to their surprise at something blocking the door, but as quickly as it started, it stopped.

I stared at my door until I fell asleep and woke the next morning with no recollection of the previous night's events or why my couch was blocking my front door. Why had I slept on it and not in my bedroom? I didn't give it much thought and went on with my day and apparently, my life. That year was 2001. I had no recollection of that night until God reminded me of it. It resurfaced one night as I was taking time to write in my journal with the goal of completing this book.

There is no doubt in my mind that at some point, Devon had drugged me and plotted with friends to come back and rape, maybe even kill, me. I can't recall if my daughter was home, but I don't believe she was. The thought of what could have happened nauseates me.

The grace, mercy, power, love, and protection of God, my Father, keeping me even in my time of sin, truly humbles me. I am here for a reason. He saved me for a reason. He kept that hidden from me for a reason, and allowed me to remember it now, for a reason. What will you choose to do with this reason?

YOUR JOURNAL

Daily we are faced with life's obstacles and trials. Things as minor as getting stuck in traffic and being late to work often cause us to become frustrated and forget the intricacy of God's map for our lives. Our sitting in traffic could have been God's very delay in protecting us from the accident that could have killed us had we been on time. Are there any moments in your life that you can turn the negative situation into the possibility of God's positivity?

CHAPTER TWELVE

Every good gift and every perfect gift is from above; it comes down from the Father of all light, in Whom there can be no variation or shadow cast by His turning.

– James 1:17

I began dating Warren in mid-2002. We were friends for five years or so prior to our dating, and I had always thought he was a good-looking, nice guy. He held a couple of jobs and though he was clearly interested in me, I never obliged him with a date. The truth of the matter is, the only reason we even began dating is because I ended up getting pregnant by him.

We were actually true friends: in the five years that I had known Warren, I had never so much as kissed him, let alone slept with him, yet our first act of promiscuity resulted in a life-long commitment to a child. Prior to our sexual relationship, we would just hang out as friends. One night in particular, after arriving home alone and realizing that it had been broken into, I called the police and then Warren. After my place was searched and reports were taken, I asked Warren to stay over with me so that I wasn't alone. His staying over wasn't uncommon, and he had always been respectful, sleeping on the couch.

This night, I suppose because I was feeling vulnerable, I asked him to sleep in my room, and after several drinks, we ended up having sex. The next day, feeling horrible about my decision, I picked an argument with him and told him that he needed to leave. He was completely confused and wanted to make things right, telling me that he wasn't the typical guy that was going to just leave me as if nothing had happened. He tried to comfort me, but I repeatedly told him to leave until he finally did. He attempted to call me, but I wouldn't answer his calls, and he finally gave up.

I didn't speak to Warren until about a month later when I ran into him at Wal-Mart. We were in the parking lot, and when I saw him, it was too late to avoid him and go another direction without showing that I was blatantly avoiding him. Warren, as he always did, stood there smiling and joking and making me laugh, as if the time that had passed was no indication of the split in our friendship. I apologized for treating him the way that I had, and we made arrangements to hang out again sometime.

Ironically enough, the next time we hung out was at my house about a week later, with me crying hysterically as I stared at the hot pink "plus" symbol on a test stick that indicated that I was pregnant. Warren and I had used a condom, but as strange as this may sound, I somehow knew from the time that we had intercourse that I was pregnant. I don't know how to put the feeling that I had into words other than to say that I felt life being conceived. It would take me the duration of my pregnancy to realize that this child was destined to be something great. As I held the positive pregnancy test, I was at my wit's end with guilt, stress, and depression.

Again, Warren tried to comfort me and promised that all would be well and even told me that he would marry me. We could get through this, he said.

Embarrassed and ashamed, I wanted to talk with my pastor about marrying Warren; I had no desire to be married to him or to anyone, for that matter. Warren just didn't seem to be an ideal husband for me: He had older children from previous relationships, and there were constant issues and even threats from his ex-girlfriend, Breanne, who didn't like me. I didn't want that within a marriage, and ultimately this was one of the underlying reasons we broke up, even after we attempted to make it work because I was pregnant.

During the initial stages of my pregnancy, I was miserable and completely ashamed of being pregnant when I was a salvation-confessed Christian. I stopped attending church. As my pregnancy grew more obvious, my shame increased. The devil drew me into such a place of deception and depression that I chose to not accept the fact that I was pregnant. I continued to drink and smoke; I never even got prenatal care or saw a physician until I was well into my sixth month.

I had stopped caring about anything and anyone, including myself. There were times that I would stay in my house, not leaving for days or answering the phone. Some days my daughter, who was now 6, would be home, and other days she would stay with her godmother.

One particular day, I remember closing all the blinds and nailing up heavy sheets and blankets to all my windows and doors so that no light would come in. It felt like I could block the world out. Nikole was home with me that day. I remember there was no food in the house because I didn't care about eating. I slept for hours until my daughter woke me up to tell me she was hungry. I finally got up and began crying as I looked around at the disheveled state of my home. I had not cared for my daughter, myself, or my unborn baby, whom I was intentionally neglecting.

I called Carrie to ask if Nikole could stay with her for awhile, and after months of not telling anyone, I told Carrie what I was going through. My business was now failing because I had no desire to work. What's more, the pregnancy put an additional strain on my body, and what little I could do was doused by the cloud of depression I faced daily with no income, unpaid bills, and final notices piled high: from my car note to the electric bill. My landlord was threatening to evict us, and I had no other place to go. Until I confessed all of this to Carrie, I had not told anyone. Friends or family would have jumped to offer assistance, but shame and embarrassment kept me silent.

On the drive to Carrie's house to drop my daughter off, I reflected on how different things had been just months earlier, and how quickly, because of my sinful actions, so much had gone so far downhill.

Less than a year earlier, I had gotten an iron-clad agreement from Taylor's, a residential rental company, to have my company consistently maintain and clean more than 200 of their homes daily, and because I cleaned for them, I was able to move into a newer, bigger home at a cheaper rate. Now, due to my current state and lack of motivation, I was being evicted from that home and had lost the contract that was given to my company.

I had been making such good money that I had purchased a new vehicle. I remember the day I had driven my red Jeep Grand Cherokee off the lot. I was so excited that I had jumped in without buckling Nikole into her car seat properly. In route, I turned around to tell her to strap herself in. "And make sure you hear the click sound it's supposed to make," I told her as she smiled back at me in the rearview mirror.

Completely satisfied that she was buckled in, I turned my attention back to the road and headed across town to show off my new vehicle to my best friend at her daycare. I looked down to pick up the built-in car phone to see if it worked, speeding along at about 50 miles per hour. I looked up just in time to see a compact car in front of me slam on its brakes, and come to a complete standstill in front of me.

"Jesus!" I shouted as I thought, "I'm going to kill everyone in that car if I slam into them." It was a little two-door car, and I was in a four-door SUV. I came screeching along at no less than 45 miles an hour as I slammed the brakes to stop, giving no thought to my surroundings. I jerked the wheel to the right, ran off the two-lane highway, and slid up the turf and dirt, now heading straight for a telephone pole. I braced myself for the crash, squeezing my eyes shut, only to open them as I felt my vehicle's front end lift off the ground, facing the heavens.

I was sitting in my front seat looking up at the sky, the rear end of my truck, wheels and all, still sitting on the ground. I had no clue what was happening until the front end of the truck began to slowly descend, slamming back to the ground and bouncing, absorbing the shock of the impact. As I stared wide-eyed out the front window, I could see the metal cable mount attached to the telephone pole and connected at the ground. My SUV had hit the cable, dead in the center, and instead of popping it, my two-ton truck simply slid up the cable like a Hot Wheel car, slid back down, and sat on the ground.

It was as if God's angel stopped it, picked it up, and sat it back down. When I snapped out of my trance, I jumped out my truck, which was now surrounded by astonished witnesses, and ran around to check on Nikole. I snatched her out of the car seat and belt that she had only buckled moments before, and began to shake as the shock of what had happened set in.

"We're okay," I told the crowd as sighs and shouts of relief came and the driver of the vehicle I'd swerved to avoid began to tear up and apologize for slamming on his brakes to avoid missing a turn and another vehicle.

"God was with you," he stated nervously as we agreed and looked at my vehicle. It had no scratches, dents, or dings, and I drove away with it in perfect operating condition.

I neared Carrie's house, reflecting on what an awesome miracle God had performed to save my life. Then just a short time later, I was contemplating dying. What a horrible, ungrateful dishonor to God, but I was convinced that I was worthless. I was exactly where satan wanted me to be.

Nikole stayed with Carrie for about a week as I began to pack up our house, expecting eviction. Carrie helped me find a small two-bedroom apartment that the landlord rented to me for less than $300 a month. He was compassionate about my having a child and being pregnant with another.

Unfortunately, less than a month later, my vehicle was repossessed, and feeling totally hopeless and helpless, I finally called my mom to ask for help moving to St. Louis. I was about 6 months pregnant at that point. I was desperate to "escape" Beaufort, believing that a new environment would be the change I needed.

I had no intention of ever coming back to Beaufort. I moved in with my parents and attempted to start a life there with no income and no vehicle. I was very dependent upon my family for help. I applied for medical, financial, and public housing assistance and began, for the first time in six months, prenatal care. Initially, and of no surprise to me, my baby was underweight but otherwise healthy, with no apparent complications.

With my mother's help, I found and moved into a two-bedroom apartment on the west side of St. Louis, right outside of downtown. It wasn't the worst part of town, but it definitely wasn't the safest either. My apartment was a two-story building with eight interior units, right off the boulevard.

There was a box at the front door for visitors to call tenants and be buzzed in. Bars lined every door and window. The sight of the bars alone made me uneasy as I wondered who needed to be kept out. That, coupled with the constant activity of what was obviously a drug house several homes away, and the crowd of loiterers who lined the street, was enough to ensure that I never left or returned home after dark.

My parents lived 20 minutes across town and even with my own place, I spent many nights with them, scared to be alone with my daughter at our apartment. As if the lack of safety there wasn't enough, there was the constant, nerve-racking stream of roaches, marijuana smoke, and arguing voices that filtered through my vents from other apartments.

I lived there for a month and a half, up until a few days after the birth of my son. Elijah was born four weeks pre-term, wide-eyed, four pounds, and healthy. He spent a week in the infant intensive care unit, comfortably sleeping in an incubator to warm his little body.

That week was the longest week of my life, as I sat looking at my baby boy, longing to take him out of his glass house and hold him. He was so tiny, and though his condition wasn't life-threatening and he was healthy overall, I felt like the worst mother ever. Depression and self-hatred set in as I dwelled on the fact that I had not properly cared for myself or my baby for the first crucial months of the pregnancy.

I had never thought of abortion as an option, but my mind went back to the place and time that I had actually contemplated and discussed giving both my children up for adoption. How could I have thought such horrible, selfish and un-motherly thoughts? It brought tears to my eyes, and I beat myself up about it for years after my son's birth.

At the same time as I struggled with this depression, I felt a strong conviction, a pull on my morals to turn from doing the wrong thing to doing the right thing. Yet again, in spite of my selfish, sinful ways, God still had a plan for me and for that tiny, prematurely born blessing of His as well.

Elijah's first name was suggested by his father, and though I didn't know it when I named him, is Hebrew, meaning "God has heard." My boy had already been brought into this world for the Greater One's purpose. His middle name, suggested by Nikole's godmother, means "God is with us." From the day he was born, Elijah had been predestined to do great things.

Seven days after his birth, we left the hospital with him weighing a little over five pounds and gaining. I returned to my apartment but moved only days later; I was increasingly concerned about my children's health due to the roach infestation that had fled from another apartment to ours as the building was being bombed and treated. Next to maggots and flies, roaches are the nastiest of terrors to me and just the sight of them, let alone the thought of them attempting to crawl on my babies or me, was enough to send me packing, even leaving behind items that I thought could be hiding the filthy things.

Back at my parents, the close quarters were unpleasant but safe, clean, and roach-free. My parents and my sister, who still lived with them, were pretty helpful with the children, initially; however, I knew this arrangement would only work for so long. With two children now, and lacking the stability and finances for a place of my own, I began to plan my return to Beaufort.

YOUR JOURNAL

Children, no matter how they were conceived or brought into this world, were all planned by God. As parents, God demands that we raise them just as the gifts they are. Parenting is not easy and no parent is perfect. Today, ask God to give you guidance in areas where you wish to be a better parent.

CHAPTER THIRTEEN

Do you not know that your body is the temple of the Holy Spirit who lives within you, whom you have received from God?
You are not your own, you were bought with a price.
So then, honor God and bring glory to Him in your body.

– 1 Corinthians 6:19-20

Only three months after moving to St. Louis, I packed what little I could fit into the backseat of a rented eight passenger Econo Van. Carrie and her friend, Shawna, had driven up from South Carolina to help me move back to Beaufort to start over again. That was 2003.

Starting over was easier said than done, as it seemed I had been stuck in the loop of "starting over" for more than two years. With my cleaning business closed and no income, I took a position in childcare again, but the pay was nowhere near enough to support my children and me on our own. We bounced from house to house, living with friends and moving five times in the course of a year.

When we left St. Louis – and each of the many times we had moved from one friend's place to another – I had left our things behind. I had no way to store our stuff; in one particular move I recall, I couldn't even move it off the street. So I stood at a nearby dumpster, angrily, thoughtlessly tossing things into it that would take up too much space in whoever else's home we would be staying in. Moving from one place to the next offered no room for my children and me, as well as our things, so slowly that year, what few things we still had were lost, stolen, left behind, or thrown out. Clothing, shoes, toys, pictures, and baby keepsakes: I kept none of it. I pretty much had nothing to hold on to but memories, and I even wished I could have thrown those out like yesterday's garbage.

During this period of moving from place to place, I still had no car and struggled financially. I had no choice but to rely upon my friends and certain men for help. Elijah's father, Warren, refused to help with any of Elijah's basic needs. Due to my leaving him and at the insistence of his ex-girlfriend, he had even resorted to claiming that there was no proof that he was the legitimate father of our child. The only time I could get Warren to pay attention to Elijah or to provide anything for him was when I would sleep with him, and even then, most times afterward he would tell me that he didn't have any money to give me for our son.

At one point, I was living with a close friend of mine, Faith, another single mother whose "deadbeat dad" seldom helped out, yet she always found a way to provide diapers, clothes, and food for both her son and mine when I couldn't. As grateful as I was, I hated seeing her struggle. It didn't seem fair to her, and my son wasn't her responsibility. Nikole's father, Malik, was consistent in paying his court-ordered child support on a monthly basis, yet it was hardly enough to split between my two children's needs as well as pay bills.

Long before I had gotten pregnant with my son, I had met "CJ" at the nightclub, but I had not seen him for years. A major drug dealer, CJ had a long-term girlfriend, and had always made it clear that he wasn't marrying her, but that he wasn't planning on leaving her either. He had no interest in dating, wining or dining me but was physically and sexually attracted to me and would "pay" for what I would give him. He was basically a modern day pimp, and short of my walking the streets, I was his whore. No need for me to sugar-coat it because that's the way it was.

Of course I didn't like it. I hated it, and I really hated myself, yet, in my time of sin – too convicted to repent and seek God – and with bills due, no food on the table or money in the bank, I convinced myself that I had no other choice. I didn't care about myself, and I allowed my body to be used as if it were void and empty. CJ handled our "transaction" with detachment, getting the service he wanted and then placing cash on the nearby dresser or table, never directly in my hand.

Lying in the bed one day after he had left, I stared at that money and became so upset and nauseated with myself and my actions that I immediately asked God for His forgiveness and never contacted or answered CJ's calls again.

Now, maybe five years later, here CJ and I were, standing in the grocery store parking lot exchanging phone numbers. The thought of our past relations disgusted me, but my struggles with money felt like a voice inside myself, cheering me on to start something with him again. We exchanged light words, and before he left, he looked at me and said to call him if I needed anything. I nodded knowingly, clearly understanding that "anything" meant his money.

After that day, I seriously contemplated calling him, thinking back on the days I was deemed trustworthy enough to go into his trunk stashed with cash and take out what I needed. But things were different now, so I really only thought of calling him for a few minutes. I had two children and wanted to get and keep my life together. What I had done with him in the past was completely disrespectful of myself and degrading. I deleted his number from my phone and never answered his calls again.

Finally, a year after I moved back to Beaufort, I was able to settle us into a place of our own when I obtained a steady, decent-paying administrative position. Things seemed to be looking up. I had redirected my life back to God, began attending church again, and had even re-opened my cleaning company. Thinking previous clients wouldn't be warm to the idea of contacting a company that had closed before, I renamed it Southern Coastal Cleaning Company and basically started from scratch. I contacted certain clients that I knew would be interested in my services again, and business began to trickle in.

The first couple of years back in Beaufort County were pretty quiet and as normal as my life had ever been. I struggled with a faithful, dedicated life to God and church as I slipped in and out of the dating and clubbing scenes.

I met Keith at a party, and if I had watched the initial signs – his demanding, persistent character and deep, intense stare – I would have seen an indication of his possessiveness. Like men always did with me, he was charming, handsome, and showered me with time, attention, and gifts at first. He was always pleasant and understanding and made it a habit to spend time with me. However, I didn't realize it then, but his frequent phone calls on the job, lunch dates, and unannounced visits to my home were flashing red signs that he was going to be trouble.

Two months into our relationship, he began to unravel. Keith had come to my daughter's birthday party, with his cousin, Derrick, to help move tables and set up. It was my first time meeting Derrick, so I was cordial and welcoming. We joked throughout the day and spoke casually, as I would with any guest in my home. Derrick was in no way threatening to Keith or flirting with me, but our conversation seemed to aggravate Keith. He became very demanding, following my every step.

When everyone left, Keith, Derrick and I were in a full blown argument with Keith cussing, fussing and yelling at me, accusing me of wanting to sleep with his cousin. Derrick defended both our characters, which only upset Keith more, until he left in a rage. Derrick and I just stood there, lost in confusion about what had just happened.

After that night, I attempted to sever ties with Keith because of his disrespect and unfounded accusations, and for just leaving me there, alone with his cousin, a stranger to me. Keith wouldn't have it, though. He refused to listen to what I had to say, and he wouldn't stop calling me. He would call my job. He would call my friends. He would even radio me on my cell phone which had walkie talkie capabilities, so I could only avoid him speaking to me over the airwaves by turning the radio off. One day I forgot to turn it off, and right in the middle of a crowded grocery store, he radioed me and began to curse and yell because I wouldn't answer or return his calls. Totally embarrassed, I scrambled to pull my phone out its holster to shut it off while onlookers stared – amazed, confused, and offended – at the crude words he loudly shouted over my radio.

He was making my life miserable, and ignoring him only fueled his fire. He would show up to my house drunk and bang on the door until I threatened to call the police. This went on for weeks until he called me, asking me to forgive him and just hear him out. Call me stupid, but I agreed, hoping he would calm down and back off if he felt like he had the upper hand. Somehow, my decision to handle the situation this way actually worked – for the first and only time.

He came over, we talked, and he moved on to his next victim. Ironically enough, Keith and I remained friends for four years after that night, until Keith got engaged and we lost touch.

After that relationship, I stopped dating for awhile, and like many times before, God focused and called my attention back to the life He had planned for me. At this point in my life, I began to recognize the patterns and signs of the devil's deception in my life. Men were not a "need" for me, but it always took just that one guy who seemed to be "The One" to grab my attention, which in turn took my focus off God. The end result was always a spiraling pathway of deception, fornication, and danger. I had never ended up with one relationship that didn't ultimately involve me or my partner battling it out, hurting each other, or acting maliciously. Every relationship I endured was just not normal, healthy, or sane at all.

Initially, not a single one of the men I dated even insinuated that they had the personalities they inevitably turned out to have. I was always drawn to the kind, sensitive, social, make-me-laugh type, but they almost always turned out to be completely opposite of that, underneath it all. I knew enough to know that every man on earth couldn't possibly be this way, so I questioned myself, my own actions, and my choice of men.

In high school, a close friend of mine had commented that I had no clue and should not be allowed to pick my own boyfriend. How close she was to the truth – even back then – that God needed to work in this area for me. Now, at a place where I wasn't sure if I could ever have a faithful, loving, healthy relationship – let alone marriage – I began to question my self-worth even more. My self-esteem dropped another notch, but back then I correlated self-esteem only with physical beauty. I didn't feel that I was ugly, but I didn't feel as pretty as some of the women around me.

I recall an ex-boyfriend, Mark, telling me that I was insecure and that I had low self-esteem because I always questioned him about whether or not he was sleeping with or seeing other women. He said that I didn't think highly enough of myself to believe or accept his compliments when he gave them. Though it hurt to hear a man tell me that I had low self-esteem, it led me to take a deeper look at the unfolding of my life's reactions to the actions of others.

Women, too, knew that I wasn't so sure of myself. In the middle of an argument, one so-called friend snidely commented about how ugly I was. Months before, while getting dressed and applying make-up, I had asked her if she thought I was pretty or not. She gave me a baffled look, thinking I was joking. "Yes," she said. "You're just looking for an ego boost!"

Now, because we were arguing, this same woman was attempting to use my insecurities against me. I knew she was being nasty and trying to hurt me, so the comment didn't affect me. Some friend.

For years, I would go back and forth in friendships with certain women who, as it would turn out, meant me nothing but harm. Some of these so called friendships were just as bad as my relationships with men were. They were persuasive enablers: ready, willing, and waiting for me to fall back into a life of clubbing, drinking, and partying, with relationships with the wrong men usually being the end result of that party girl lifestyle.

One sin led to another, and the devil had me hook, line, and sinker. After awhile, my partying was so out of control that I just did not care how drunk I got, who saw me acting wild, or what guy I left with. Drinking became a routine thing at least once or twice a week, and getting men became a game. The nightclub was a place any woman could go and get all the attention she wanted. Though the club guys' interest in me wasn't genuine, and I was rarely safe, with my low self-esteem and lack of confidence, I almost believed the partying and everything after it empowered me.

YOUR JOURNAL

Disrespecting our bodies is one of the greatest acts of dishonor to God and to ourselves. Fornication – the act of sex outside of marriage – is sinful to God and an injustice to what we deserve to preserve. Though we can't change the past, we can control our future. Write out all the reasons you feel you would benefit from postponing any acts until marriage. What do you seek to gain when you willingly give yourself for the purpose of sex?

CHAPTER FOURTEEN

For if you forgive people their trespasses, their reckless and willful sins, leaving them, letting them go, and giving up resentment, your heavenly Father will also forgive you

– Matthew 6:14

After months of clubbing, nightlife, drinking, and partying, the usual end result was a meaningless, empty relationship with some good-for-nothing guy. This time was no different on the surface, but once I had gotten closer to Mark, I was exposed to a totally different world of demons than I had never known before.

I met Mark while hanging out with friends in Savannah, Georgia. He lived in Beaufort and knew most of the girls I was with, but we had never met. The attraction was instant, and the chemistry seemed perfect as we laughed, talked, and danced all night. We exchanged numbers, and then spent almost every day together.

It felt too good to be true: there were never any arguments, no cheating or lies. He was great with my kids, and I adored his. All of us often did things together, and it felt as if we were a family. He was a good guy, but the closer we became, the more comfortable Mark was with exposing me to his true lifestyle. Not only did he smoke marijuana, he sold it as well. Months into our relationship, I found this out as he nonchalantly opened his front door and made a sale as I sat quietly, shocked at what he was doing.

"It's for a friend," he reassured me. "I'm just helping him get rid of it. If you don't like me doing it, I won't anymore."

I *didn't* like it, but that didn't stop him, and our relationship became strained as we argued about his attempts to hide what he was doing. After another couple of months, the relationship ended. Mark was distant, hard to find when I needed him, unable to ever keep his word, and increasingly spacey and paranoid.

A few weeks after we broke up, he called to talk. He said he wasn't feeling well and just wasn't himself. He was depressed and upset, a pattern I had began to notice before we had broken up. He came over that night, and as I slept, he tossed and turned, getting up throughout the night to pace from the bedroom to the bathroom and back again.

Finally, when I got up in the morning to go to work, he had fallen asleep. I walked into the bathroom to shower and stopped, frozen as I stared at the sink. Never in my life had I done cocaine, or even seen it, but everything within me screamed that this was what it was. It all made so much sense now: Mark's paranoia, his bloodshot eyes, his lack of care and concern, the depression, and the fact that he had been in and out of the bathroom all night.

I could feel my heart pounding and blood rushing in my ears. I was angry and fearful. I didn't know what to do or what to say to him. I didn't know how he would react because I didn't even know who he was anymore. I closed the door and locked myself in the bathroom as I tried to come up with a rational explanation for what I was seeing, but the more I reflected, the more obvious it was.

My mind went back to a particular night at his work place, where he was the manager of a local convenience store; we sat in the break room talking while he pointed out grooves on the table top. He said they were cuts from razors used from other employees "making lines."

My mind raced through the numerous occasions when he had expressed some sort of knowledge about cocaine to me, and I had completely paid it no attention. My anger softened as I began to worry about him. Or was he trying to pull me into his world?

I didn't want to face the facts right then and there. I quickly dusted up the fine powder with a piece of tissue, flushed it down the toilet, and got ready for work.

As the days went by, I paid more attention to Mark's actions and moods. It didn't take long to confirm my assumptions. Initially, he blew off my questioning him and continued to insist that the cocaine he was selling was to benefit a friend, but he was making money along the way as well. At this point, he openly purchased, weighed and bagged his product, even if I was around, and he didn't seem concerned that I wanted nothing to do with his lifestyle.

Mark had many tell-tale signs of substance abuse: his obvious lifestyle change, loss of weight, and sketchy moods. The biggest sign that he was an addict, though, was that even though he was selling drugs, he never had any money to show for it. He was doing more coke than he was selling, which only led to deeper debt and harsher problems.

Though we never resumed dating, a part of me cared deeply for him, and I hated what was happening to him, so I tried to help when and where I could, later realizing that I was only enabling him. I allowed Mark to use my vehicle for so-called "job interviews" and "picking his children up for visitation" but later found all those incidents were lies. He lied to me and stole from me and simply was no longer himself. Finally, I'd had enough and just gave up and chose to sever ties altogether.

However, even that turned out to be easier said than done. That summer I had acquired a second car and had offered Mark the use of one of mine so he could get to and from his job. When I chose to end communication with him, he went into hiding ... with my car. He wouldn't answer his phone or return my calls.

Frustrated and without options, I eventually called the police to file a stolen vehicle report. Even their attempts to contact Mark met with no response. Finally, I was able to track him down. I had to argue with his new girlfriend, and nearly got in a physical fight with her, but at last I got my car back. It was in her garage, and all along he had told her it was his, so when I showed up, she was very defensive.

After that night, I had no more contact with Mark; however, for all my time, friendship, and care, he showed his gratitude later that summer by slashing every tire on the Lexus I was driving, which belonged to a friend of mine. He made it clear that he was the one who had done it by leaving the entire blade of an Exacto knife – from his stockroom job – in the front driver's side tire. He had always carried one. I had not seen or talked to Mark for months, but apparently he had been watching me, waiting for revenge, or maybe he was upset that I was driving another man's car.

At this point, I began to take a long, hard look at my life and the people in it. All I had ever wanted was true love, honesty, integrity, and peace. I was fed up with the continuous cycle of abusive, lying, cheating men I had dated. Even some of the women I knew were just too much for me anymore; they gossiped, stabbed me in the back, and even slept with my cheating, abusive, junkie so-called boyfriends.

I withdrew from friends and became even angrier as I revisited thoughts of the molestation in my childhood. It was as if the memory just came back in full force, slamming the forefront of my thoughts. Early one morning, I woke up and just lay in bed, boiling with rage at all the thoughts of things that had been said and done to me by my family. I was angry with the world. I didn't curse God, but back then, I didn't and *couldn't* see His marvelous plan, and I despised myself and my life.

I felt helpless, hopeless, and unwanted. At 27 years old, with my life really just beginning, I felt as if it were over. I was a single mother with two kids from two different men, low self-esteem, no self-confidence, and had been pushed down, beaten up, and kicked around by the world. Who could or would possibly want me with all that physical and emotional baggage in tow? For a moment, the world made me bitter and mean. I despised all those who had ever wronged or hurt me, but even worse, I neglected, shut out or despised all of those who *did* truly care for me and had never done a thing to me. Certain friends – true friends – for reasons only God could allow, dealt with me, prayed for me, and still loved me despite my harsh and selfish ways.

I recall crying to my best friend and telling her how much I wanted to be hateful and hurtful to everyone who had hurt me and even to people in general. I was crying because I was frustrated that I couldn't do those things.

"You don't have the heart for that, Takiya," she told me. "That's not who God made you to be, so you *won't* be that way." She was right. My bouts of anger – lashing out at others, even cussing them out – were always followed by sincere apologies, compassion, and repentance.

At that time, and even more so now, I just couldn't, wouldn't, and *will* not hold a grudge, seek revenge, or not forgive, no matter what someone says or does to me. However, looking back, as great as my character was, I had not yet walked into the truth of "forgiveness." My way of dealing with pain was to simply forget; however, forgetting was the key ability that often led me back to the starting point of a lot of things, places and people God had moved me away from.

For a year or so after my fiasco with Mark, I spent time just working and being alone. My friend Walter and I hung out from time to time, but it definitely wasn't a dating thing. I had known Walter for six or seven years at this point, and though he had always expressed an interest in me, I had never entertained the thought of a relationship with him. I was not comfortable with the idea because he was twenty years my senior and actually a year older than both of my parents. While I didn't look at him as a father figure, he was very caring, nurturing and protective toward my children and me.

Elijah, who was now two years old, and Nikole, now eight, loved having him around. They had grown up around him, and while Elijah's father chose not to be in their lives, Walter happily filled in. He would play games with them, shop for them, and attempt to cook for them. He even helped potty train Elijah. He was always there, always helpful, and for all that he did for them, he did five times more for me.

It wasn't until I really started paying attention to Walter's interaction with my kids that I realized how much he had been there for me through the years. He never judged, never pestered, but was always there to offer his shoulder, smile, or time. For years this man had watched me suffer from one relationship to the next, struggling and battling with man after man, but he never complained, compared himself to them, or stopped being my friend.

I have to admit that, again, because of the age difference, I had never really focused whole-heartedly on being his friend. To me, he was a "dirty old man" that I could use for what I wanted and needed financially without having to give up anything in return. I took advantage of his kindness. But then, coming home from work one day, I walked in on my daughter and him playing the board game "Candy Land," and I began to wonder "what if."

Walter had dropped everything when he had gotten my last-minute call to babysit the kids for me. He had successfully put Elijah down for a nap, and Nikole was giggling excitedly as she played the board game with him. That moment was picture perfect to me, and from then on, I decided that if anyone cared about me and the kids, it was Walter. If anyone wanted the best for us, it was Walter. If ever there was a provider and protector for us, it was Walter. If ever there was a man who would love me, cherish me, and be faithful to me, it was Walter.

Suddenly, his age didn't mean a thing to me. I was 28 and he was 48, but he didn't even look his age. I began to pay more attention to him and noticed things about him that were attractive. After years of expressing an interest in me, but never pursuing a relationship, he didn't even realize that my heart and mind were changing toward him. For months, we continued to be friends without my saying a word. I was nervous about damaging our friendship, and I worried about people's thoughts about our age difference: specifically my parents'.

Finally, about a week before Christmas, after we had taken a shopping trip for the kids together, I asked him why he did so much for the kids and me. Walter said everything that I could possibly want to hear. He said he was in love with me and had been for years. He said that he had painfully watched me get into bad relationships and wished that he would have had the courage to speak up and let me know how he felt about me.

I finally told him how I had been feeling for months, as I had begun to realize how much he cared for my children and me. I said that I was sorry that I had ever neglected to see his feelings for me but now I wanted to give us a chance. He didn't believe me at first, but we talked more and officially started dating, right around Christmas.

I was happy, he was happy, and the kids were happy. There was no drama, no arguments, lies or cheating. Some people, especially my friends, couldn't understand what I saw in him or why I was dating a much-older man, but I didn't care. Our relationship lacked the gossipy, twisted, game-playing night life that I had dealt with so often. It appeared to others that we were boring, but I loved it. He wanted my time and attention and took an interest in the things I desired. He wanted to take care of me, and I wanted to be taken care of. He appreciated every simple detail about me and never went long without giving me a compliment. Making me smile was what he did best, and I loved him so much for it. Most of all, I loved him for loving me.

YOUR JOURNAL

Oftentimes, the act of forgiving is associated with having to forget or trust, and most people cannot balance out the two, thus allowing a lack of forgiveness to fester. Over the years, I have had to learn that it is essential to forgive, but it is actually wise to not forget. Forgetting can lead us back to the very place from which we were delivered. What things are you trying to forget in order to move on, but still find unforgivable?

CHAPTER FIFTEEN

And my God will liberally supply, fill to the full, your every need according to His riches in glory in Christ Jesus
– Philippians 4:19

Three months later, in March, Walter took me car shopping for my birthday, and I picked out the cutest little red four-door Lexus GS. No man had ever really given me anything and definitely not a car. The day we signed the paperwork on it, I completed the documents in my name as the owner, listing Walter only as the insurance carrier; the car and title were completely mine. The car was purchased a few days prior to my birthday, so Walter took it to get it detailed and have maintenance done, and on my birthday, he showed up to present it to me. He had added some custom features, a new graphic CD player, the works.

I couldn't believe how well our relationship was going, how happy we were, and how much he seemed to care about me. Walter made money so easily – by selling illegal copies of digital music and movies – that spending it wasn't an issue. The money came as quickly as it went. I heard rumors later that he had once been a big time drug dealer, years before we had ever met, but I never saw any evidence of that. My closet was full of clothes, shoes, and designer handbags from our shopping trips to Atlanta and New York City. He paid all the bills, made sure I always had money, and never left the children out of anything. He gave them anything and everything their hearts desired. My daughter even gained his passion for foreign luxury cars and would often go with him to car shows or help him detail and show off his cars.

My son, on his own, began calling Walter "Dad," but my nervousness about this quickly calmed when I noticed how much it melted Walter's heart to hear Elijah say that. Everywhere he went, he showed off his "son" so much that word got back to Elijah's totally uninvolved father, who was annoyed and jealous. What a joke!

At this time, I was active in church, and to all appearances, all was well and I was happy, but spiritually I wasn't giving or living my all for God. My own desires were leading me, and even though we were not living together at this point, Walter and I were "in sin." I still drank, I still had sex, and I still cussed and lived in a worldly way.

About four months into our relationship, shortly after my birthday, the unthinkable happened. Early one morning, about a week after Easter, Walter and I had our first argument, about us attending church. I had made it clear that we needed to go to church on a regular basis and begin to build a spiritual foundation in our relationship. He had argued and insisted that I visit his church first and then he would attend mine. The day we visited my church, as usual the entire congregation was prompted to leave their seats and come up to the altar for corporate worship. As everyone began leaving their seats, I waited for Walter, who was standing at my right side, to exit our aisle and head to the altar. He didn't move, and as I tapped his arm and gestured for him to move out, he mouthed the word "No."

At that point, I figured he was unclear about what was going on and whispered to him: "Everyone is going up." He glared at me and again said "No." Still confused by his actions, I pressed in front by him, stepped out into the aisle, and reached for his hand reassuringly to lead him out. My compassionate attempt was rudely halted as he tightened his grip on my hand and jerked me back towards him. He glared at me again and angrily muttered "No" again.

For the rest of the service, I sat quietly, in shock at both his defiance and the physical reprimand, in church of all places. Riding back home, I listened silently as Walter told me that he wasn't going to be made to do something he didn't want to do. He said he would only go to church when, where, and if he wanted to. At that moment, everything within me knew that our relationship needed to end.

Back at Walter's house, I attempted again to let him know how important church was to me, but the more we talked, the angrier he became. I began to see a side of him that I never knew existed. He spoke roughly to me, ignored me when he felt what I said didn't warrant a response, and even raised his voice to talk over me and shut me up. He didn't care about what I cared about, and pretty much told me I had to choose either him or church.

About a week went by. Neither of us bothered to call or visit the other. He went on with his life as usual, as I did with mine. Finally, we passed each other while driving one day and pulled over to talk. Walter was remorseful about what he'd said and done, and said that he was sorry and missed me.

I wasn't so moved, myself, though I had missed him, too. I told him that I needed some time to myself and wasn't sure about our relationship anymore. His sorrow quickly turned to anger, and he sped off in frustration.

I didn't like being hurt, I didn't like being disrespected, and I didn't like how easily his affection toward me could shift. These were all warning signs that spoke loud and clear, yet only a day or two later, I decided I wanted to work on our relationship because I thought I loved him. I believed that, with time, he'd change.

One morning, after dropping my kids off at school, I decided to go over and surprise him by making him breakfast. I had a key to his house, but from a previous experience, I would always call to let him know that I was coming in so that I wouldn't startle him. Walter slept deeply, and being caught off guard sent him into a panic.

Halfway to his house, I called but got no answer. As I pulled into his driveway, I called him again, just as he was rushing out his front door. I wasn't even out of the car by the time he approached me. I got out, gave him a hug, and asked where he was going so early. He had a vacuum cleaner in his hand, and as I stepped away, I noticed how frantic and sweaty he looked.

He rambled on about going "over there," as he pointed toward a row of houses but not to anywhere specific. He was blocking my path as I walked toward the front door, then he took my hand and told me to go "over there" with him. At that point I realized he was up to something and didn't want me to go in the house.

"Okay, I'll go with you, but first I really have to use the bathroom," I lied. I walked around him and headed for the porch.

"Baby?" he called as he grabbed my arm and positioned himself in my path again.

"What?" I snapped, as I narrowed my eyes, clenched my jaw, and snatched my arm away from him.

"Please come go with me," he whispered as his eyes began to well up with tears. I just stared at him and shook my head in disgust and disbelief.

"You have someone else in that house, don't you?" I demanded.

Tears rolled down his cheeks, and he dropped his head as he whispered, "Yes." I pushed past him and again started towards the front door. I made it to the porch and got my hand on the door knob just as Walter came barreling up the stairs and pushed in front of me. He began yelling, telling me to go home, and that he would handle it.

I was furious that he would send me home and try to protect the identity of this other person, whom I assumed was another woman.

Surprisingly, in spite of all the shouting, struggling, and my banging on the window, no one else ever appeared.

Walter began cursing me and calling me every name that came to his mind. Then he picked me up and shoved me down the porch stairs. I was so shocked that I began to cry and ask him why he was doing this to me, but he was beyond the point of rage. I don't think he heard my words nor did he care. I dusted myself off, got in my car, and sped off so angrily that I nearly hit the house behind me.

For days after that, I went through a roller coaster of emotions. I was hurt, angry, confused, disappointed, and disgusted. Why would he do this to me? *How* could he do this to me? I even felt as if he couldn't possibly have found another woman who would want him. I was the best woman he could ever get: I was 20 years younger than he was, smart, beautiful, and a good girl. "How dare him!" I thought.

Pretty soon, though, I was judging myself harshly, as usual, thanks to this latest crushing blow to my self-esteem. If I couldn't keep the faithful attention of an older, plain-looking man, then what was wrong with *me*?

Depression set in, and for days I couldn't eat, sleep, or go out in public. The fact that Walter was the one who'd done wrong became obscured by my feelings of worthlessness, and I began to miss him. I was convinced that I must have upset and misled him. I must have expected too much, too soon regarding church. Maybe all of this was my fault.

Eventually, I called him. I was confident that he at least missed me and would be glad to hear my voice. He would probably be ready to talk and work all of our issues out.

"Yeah, what?" he asked when he answered the phone. I was caught off-guard by his tone and didn't know what to say, but as I began to talk, his tone and voice warmed up as he realized that I wasn't calling for a fight.

I didn't really know what to say or where to begin, so I mentioned that he still had some handbags of mine from our recent shopping trip to New York. I asked him if he could bring them when he was nearby. He agreed, and I rushed to dress myself up.

I don't recall how much time went by, but eventually I called to see if he was okay, because he should have made it to me at this point. He answered the phone just as gruffly as he had before. I asked him if he was still coming.

"Your things are at the front door," he snapped. "I already came and dropped them off."

"What?" I asked. I got off the couch and opened the front door. Then I shouted at Walter as I stared at my designer handbags sitting on my front step for anyone to take. "Why would you do that? What were you thinking?" I demanded.

"I don't want to see you," was his response. "If I came in to see you, you'll just start crying, and we'll get back together. I just don't want this drama and headache with you." Then he hung up on me.

My depression and sense of worthlessness was quickly replaced with anger and a state of defiance towards Walter. I went through my apartment –one which he had signed for and was paying the bills for – and began taking down and packing up all of his things. We didn't live together, but he had plenty of things there, as if he did. I didn't tear, rip or bleach things; he still had other items of mine that I wanted back.

I neatly folded and boxed his things, called him, and told him to meet me at the nearby gas station to get them. When we met, I attempted to be cordial as he pushed me out of his way to get his things and place them in his trunk. As I was gathering smaller items of mine out of his car, I repeated a conversation that I had earlier that week with his ex-girlfriend and told him that I knew who had been in his house that day because I had personally called his ex-girlfriend, and we had talked. When I told him that I had gotten her number off his cell phone bill, he cursed me, threw his car in reverse, and slammed his foot on the gas. I just barely missed being hit by the open door and dragged underneath the car because I was still leaning inside the passenger's side.

I hit the ground flat, and a store clerk who had witnessed the scene came rushing out to see if I was okay. Walter, who didn't even look back, sped off with the passenger side door open. I told the clerk I was okay as he helped me into my car. I drove home in tears. I could have been seriously hurt or killed, and he didn't even care.

Several days later, Walter contacted me to talk and apologize. Because I was still blaming myself, I listened to his emotional spiel about how much he missed me and how upset he was about hurting me. We ended up agreeing to work things out and to put the current incidents behind us.

However, things weren't the same. Trust was no longer there, so we began to argue a lot. Even though I attempted to make up excuses for his past behavior, or tried to believe him when he attempted to explain his actions, deep down I knew that I couldn't. I just didn't want to deal with him anymore. Walter's position as a bouncer at a local nightclub required him to work late; the fact that he also had to interact with women didn't inspire me to trust him.

One evening, after we had an argument over the phone, I went to Walter's house to pack any of my remaining things. All we ever did at this point was argue, and we both were fed up and tired. He treated me so cruelly on a regular basis: ignoring my phone calls whenever he felt like it, never offering any explanation of who was at his house that day that I'd caught him cheating. He basically blew me off and made it clear that I could deal with him his way, take it or leave it.

He threatened me one night at dinner. My children were with us and out of nowhere, he calmly leaned across the table, looked me in the eye, and told me, "If you ever leave me, I'll kill you." Then he leaned back and continued his meal.

The statement was so bizarre and irrelevant to anything that was going on between us. I wasn't sure how to take him. The thought of his being serious frightened me, yet it was so shocking that I never spoke up or asked him if he was serious or not.

So there I was, at his house packing my things, calmly attempting to communicate with him as he went on ironing his clothes and getting dressed, ignoring me as if I wasn't even there. He was getting ready to go to the race track, and I knew he planned to take or meet some woman. Even though I was leaving him, it bothered me so much that he had threatened so nonchalantly to kill me if I did, yet he had plenty of women at the ready to replace me or anyone else who didn't see or do things his way.

It didn't bother him to see me cry, it didn't move him to know he had hurt me, and he never stopped to think twice about cursing me out or degrading me with horrible names. Though he ignored everything *I* said, he picked up the phone and began a conversation with the woman he was going to meet.

My pain turned to anger as I stood at his bedroom door. He turned to face me while he talked to this woman, and something inside me exploded. I flew into a rage and started throwing things off his dresser, tearing up anything I could, trying to express how I was feeling. I began yelling and cursing him, and he immediately ran toward me with his hand in the air. Afraid that I would have to fight him off me, I punched him in the face. He stopped, and the blow that I braced myself for never came. He backed up, shocked, and stared at me. He began to curse me out and tell me that I was going to jail.

I cried, pleading with him not to call the police as he dialed 911. I'd hit him out of fear and in reaction to the way he had lunged at me and he knew it. I begged him to think about my kids and told him that I was sorry, but my pleading only fueled his cruelty and anger towards me. He began to mock and curse me, repeatedly saying "Oh, yeah, you're going to go to jail today!"

He tried to grab me to make me stay, but I quickly darted outside. I didn't know what to do or where to go because I didn't even have my car over at his house, and I knew he'd report it as stolen if I got back in his car. I left walking to the house of a friend who lived nearby. Walter sent the cops over to her house. They took my story and told me they were arresting me because I had broken his eye glasses when I had hit him, and he was cut up and bleeding pretty badly.

Handcuffed and in the back seat of the cruiser, I cried silently at the lengths Walter had gone to in order to see that I was arrested and that charges were pressed. No matter how angry I'd gotten, I'd had no right to damage his things, and though I'd hit him, it was in self-defense. But the one thing I didn't do was break his eyeglasses! He wasn't wearing them when I hit him, and the ones that he had given the cops as proof were an old broken pair that had been sitting in his kitchen window sill for weeks, which I had even previously attempted to help him fix.

At the detention center, I felt so numb, alone, and lost. I was allowed to make phone calls, but I had no clue who to call. I was ashamed of the path my life was on. A friend made sure my kids were cared for, and I spent the night in jail for the third time in my life, after another relationship had gone wrong and I had, yet again, made terrible choices.

YOUR JOURNAL

In John 14:6, Jesus says that He is the way, the truth and the life. Can you imagine your life being any different than the state it is in right now? Suppose you are facing some giant obstacle such as a physical or verbal abuse, low self-esteem, or depression. What would your life be like if you could have it all wiped away this very instant?

CHAPTER SIXTEEN

You shall not need to fight in this battle; take your positions, stand still, and see the deliverance of the Lord who is with you, O Judah and Jerusalem. Fear not nor be dismayed. Tomorrow go out against them, for the Lord is with you.

– 2 Chronicles 20:17

The next morning, I was sent before the judge. The day before, the two police officers had made it clear that I was the one who was wrong, and there would be consequences to my actions. They had even stood laughing and joking with Walter while I sat in the car waiting. But the judge was different. I sat across from him, quietly, head and eyes down, waiting for him to seal my fate and charge me. I awaited his reprimand and rough tone, but it never came.

"You don't belong here," he stated as he read over the paperwork. "Why are you here?" I described the events, confessing my faults and taking the blame, but he responded as if he could see through every bit of emotional and physical abuse I had ever put up with. He patiently explained that whether or not I thought a man *meant* to hurt me or not, if he shoved me but didn't punch, that it was still physical abuse, and I didn't deserve it. He told me to stop making excuses for Walter and asked me if I was scared of Walter or needed to talk to a victim's advocate. At this time in my life, I couldn't wrap my mind around the fact that I was being categorized as "one of those women in an abusive relationship," but the more he talked and questioned me, the clearer it became that I was just that woman.

The judge made a phone call, referred me to an abuse advocate counselor, and basically dropped my charges, telling me to call him at his office directly for anything I might need. Then he gave orders for me to be released.

Over the following days, I let the judge's words sink in. He had told me that I was making excuses for Walter when he had "just" pushed me. Realizing that I had been physically abused – and that others could see it when I couldn't – was sickening to me. Disappointed with myself and disgusted by Walter, I met with a court advocate and began to revisit my relationship with God for the first time in months. I again asked God for His forgiveness for all my past actions and sins, and easily focused on God, not Walter.

I was working as a legal assistant and made my own money, so with Walter out of the picture, I easily took over paying my own bills and making payments on the car. He had made it clear that it was mine, and the title and bill of sale were both in my name. However, we had placed the car on his insurance policy, and for the sake of being allowed to add me to his policy, I had opted to write his name in the upper corner of the bill of sale.

Walter never signed any documents of ownership, but at some point, he must have taken all of this into consideration because weeks later he somehow had a duplicate key made, showed up at my apartment late one night, and took the car without ever asking or telling me he was going to do so.

Earlier that day, I had gone to dinner and a movie with a friend. I got home and went up to the apartment's third floor to pick up my kids from a friend who was watching them. I sat and chatted with her for about thirty minutes, then left to go to my first floor apartment. As I walked inside, within myself, but not knowing it was God at the time, I heard the words, "Go check on your car." I hesitated because it made no sense, but I decided it would do no harm to go look and make sure the doors were locked and lights were out.

Walking back toward the parking lot, I came around the corner and found an empty space where I had just parked my car only a half hour before. I blinked and stared at the empty spot and even checked a few other spaces, thinking I must have parked elsewhere. After it all sank in, I knew it had to be Walter who had taken my car.

I went in the house and called his cell phone repeatedly, but of course he never answered. Finally, I called the police to file a report. This was only the beginning of his terror and deceit.

I didn't get my car back that night, and Walter wouldn't answer phone calls from me or the police. Walter knew that I needed the car to transport my kids to and from school, as well as get to work. The next morning, I relied on a neighbor to get my kids to school. I missed a day of work at the law office and rescheduled clients for the weekend among my recently reestablished cleaning clientele. I felt certain that I would have my car back by then. I didn't think for one minute that Walter would jeopardize my life, once he rationally thought things through.

It turned out I was as wrong as ever: one day turned into two, then days turned into weeks, and weeks turned into months without my car.

The police were unable to locate either the car or Walter, and my frustrations seemed never-ending: I had no reliable transportation to work, so I lost my job. I couldn't get to my cleaning clients, so I had to put that business on hold, not to mention that most of my supplies, equipment, and linen were in the trunk of the car he had taken. My daughter, who was about 9 at the time, was on medication and needed regular breathing treatments from a nebulizer machine that was still in the car. Walter knew all of this, yet he still refused to have compassion.

My neighbor continued to see that my children made it to school, but other than that, I sat home day in and day out with nothing to do and no way to get anywhere. With no income, my savings quickly dwindled. Every bill was past due, and we faced the prospect of all our utilities being disconnected. I had received an eviction notice, and to top it off, I was getting payment demand notices for a car I no longer had.

Walter was the policy holder for the insurance on it, so I wasn't legally authorized to file any claims on the vehicle. Due to my making one simple decision – to write Walter's name on the contract regarding insurance – the police now made it clear that the car "technically" wasn't stolen, and both of us had legal rights to it. Even worse, my sole proof of ownership – the bill of sale – would turn out to be questionable months later when I took Walter to court for the car and my belongings.

It felt as though my world was crumbling away. With everything I had being taken from me, I began to seek God. I clearly remember being assured that God wouldn't let Walter defeat me. Certain members of my church saw to it that I had a ride to Sunday service and Bible study. Daily, I began to spend more time in prayer and reading the Bible. I clung to every word that God was teaching through my pastor, and I kept confidence in God.

Through the struggle, there were plenty of days that I cried, but God took me to a place of supernatural faith. I had hit rock bottom, but in my faith all wasn't lost. I knew that God was going to see to it that I was taken care of.

Friends couldn't believe that I felt okay, and neighbors were astonished when I cheerfully gave away and blessed them with most of my home's contents the day I was officially evicted. I was at such a place of peace that I think people believed I was silently losing my mind. At times, I myself wondered how I had become so assured of my safety, sanity, and peace. It truly was amazing to be at such a place.

I saw Walter for the first time in months at the court hearing for my punching him on the day we had broken up. He showed up with his current girlfriend and actually had the nerve to try to use her as a key witness to my punching him. The judge quickly and sternly dismissed her from the courtroom, as it was apparent that both Walter and his girlfriend were lying.

Walter's integrity was now questionable, and his entire story was disregarded by the judge. I was, however, charged with injury to personal property, for knocking things off his dresser, and ordered to pay $50. There were no other repercussions due to my previously having spent the night in jail. Before we were dismissed, I brought up the issue of my car but was told that one case had nothing to do with the other and that we would need another court date.

After I requested to at least be given my things that were in the car, the judge furiously demanded that Walter go outside and bring me all that was mine, including Nikole's medication. Escorted by an officer, he returned with a garbage bag full of items, most of them damaged.

The judge exploded when Walter walked in with my son's car seat, and spoke harshly to him about his neglect of my children's needs. I couldn't help but bow my head to hide my giggles. As a hush fell over the courtroom, the judge continued, telling Walter how pathetic he was for stealing from my children and me, as well as attempting to make himself look like the victim by fraudulently falsifying legal documents.

Walter was furious, denying that he had ever had a relationship with me. He then went on to state that he didn't even know that I had children. Just then, the judge was holding a picture, taken on Christmas day, of Walter and my son. By the close of the court hearing, the judge had made it clear that I needed to stay away from Walter. She had even recalled having him in her court before for a similar case in which he and his wife at the time also had issues over a car and home that he had purchased for her, then took back and destroyed. I was finding out more and more that Walter was no stranger to the criminal system.

The kids and I were now living with a friend. Back at her place, I began to research the county files to look further into Walter's history of attendance in court. Walter – whose name I later found out wasn't even Walter – was a liar, a thief, and a murderer. By his account, he later told me that he had beaten a murder charge by claiming self-defense.

His stealing my car was nothing new, as well. According to county police reports, he had done exactly the same thing to his wife, whom he had initially told me was his ex-wife, after they had been separated for awhile. Fear gripped me as I remembered that night over dinner when he'd threatened to kill me; I wasn't sure what he was capable of, or how far he would go to hurt me, but God quickly reassured me that I had nothing to fear.

Prior to our court date about my car, Walter gave it to his new girlfriend to drive around town. I pulled into McDonalds one day, hopped out of my friend's car that she had loaned me, and ran inside to grab a meal. When I came back out, I noticed a car was parked behind me, blocking me in. When I looked in my rearview mirror, I saw *my* red Lexus GS.

I turned around to see who was in the driver's seat, but it was empty. I sat baffled and unsure what to do, certain that whoever was driving it had seen me pull up and intentionally blocked me in so that I could see him or her.

For a moment, I thought about hopping into it and driving off. I still had my set of keys, but quickly decided against it. At this point, months had gone by: in passing I had already seen another woman driving it, and court was just days away. I had made up my mind that I no longer wanted the car but was going to seek reimbursement for payments I had made to the finance company, up until Walter had stolen it. I sat there, patiently eating my fries and waiting for some random woman to come back to get the car out of my way so that I could leave.

Later, after many attempts to have a processor serve Walter a court summons, I finally had my day in court. The same judge who had presided over our previous case was present and listened with an obvious disdain to the barrage of lies that Walter spoke as he made every effort to belittle, disrespect, and demean anything about me and my character. Walter continued to deny that we had dated, and claimed not to know my kids or any of my friends that I had brought as witnesses that day. He even brought several of his friends who didn't know the truth about why we were there. They were quickly dismissed from testifying as Walter attempted to push them into lying for him.

For the duration of the hearing, I sat quietly and only spoke when prompted to and presented material and documentation when necessary. I had truly given the situation over to God and asked Him to go before me as my defense. Walter stumbled and stammered over so many of his lies that I almost felt sorry for him. He was making himself look like a fool, and even the friends he brought to defend him were telling him to shut up and giving me apologetic and compassionate looks.

While he was testifying, the mechanic who had done some work on the vehicle looked from Walter to the judge and stated that he wasn't going to jeopardize himself and lie for Walter. Walter's most pathetic move was to submit a newly printed, freshly forged copy of the car's bill of sale. Days before the car had been stolen from me, God kept prompting me to remove important documents, such as the bill of sale, from the glove box. I kept forgetting to do so, but just hours before Walter stole the car, I had removed the bill of sale, title, and some other personal documents that proved my ownership of the vehicle.

For weeks I had called and visited the dealership, seeking their help in proving that I was the rightful owner of the car, yet the owner of the dealership was a close friend of Walter's, and had only ignored me or disputed my claim. Now in court, I was certain that Walter felt I had no proof as he boldly handed his forged copy to the judge. The owner of the dealership, as Walter stated, had given him proof of his copy, but wasn't present to testify that day in court.

The judge snickered as she looked back and forth from his copy to mine, then called me up to review them.

"Is this your signature?" she asked.

I barely got out, "No, ma'am," before she sat back, glared at Walter, and said, "I didn't think so."

Walter continued to deny the truth of the matter and grew short-tempered with the judge. I sat quietly and just began to pray and praise God within myself as she dealt with him. The owner of the dealership whom Walter said was coming, to no one's surprise, didn't show and couldn't be reached.

By the end of court, Walter was furious and continued to plead his case for the car. However, when the judge asked, I told her that I no longer wanted the car back. Shocked, Walter's head snapped in my direction and his eyes widened. I had long let go of the desire to keep the car. He had stolen it from me, given it to another woman, and I had no need for it. I did, however, want back the money I had invested into the car, as well as my name legally and properly removed from its title of ownership. At this point, I still didn't have any transportation and was counting on reimbursement of the funds so that I could purchase another vehicle and get back to work.

Some things in life are truly priceless and the "man tantrum" that he threw when the judge ordered him to pay me for the car he had bought was one of them. Tears of joy streamed down my cheeks as I lowered my head and giggled into my chest. From the court house to the parking lot, I praised God and hugged my friends.

As we stood outside talking, I noticed Walter and his friends drive up and stop only a few feet away from where we were standing. At first I paid no attention to him, but as he sat there in the driver's seat, I couldn't help overhearing his friends pleading with him about something. "Oh my God, this man is going to shoot me or run me over," I thought. When my friends noticed, too, we all got in our cars and left.

Walter had thirty days to respond with payment by certified mail, but he didn't do it immediately. He waited the entire time, so right at thirty days, I received payment.

YOUR JOURNAL

Seeking revenge on others for wrongs done to us may be our first instinct, yet God tells us that doing things His way is a better way. When we allow God to fight our fights, the battle is never lost. What battles do you need God to fight for you?

CHAPTER SEVENTEEN

Pride goes before destruction and a haughty spirit before a fall.
– Proverbs 16:18

A little while later, I was able to give my testimony about this entire ordeal and God's deliverance to the congregation at my church. At this point in my life, I felt so good, finally knowing what it truly meant to love God. I had a real relationship with Him, and I could feel and see the plans He had for me unfolding.

As I stood in front of the church that day, I saw the hopeful faces of many young women looking back at me and clinging to the words of my testimony. I saw the smiling faces of my church family, those who had prayed for and encouraged me, even in times of my not-so-faithful state. I remember the tears streaming down the faces of several of the married women, whose hearts I know held a silent prayer for the man God truly had chosen for me. I remember the praises going up from both men and women, as we all gave God the glory for the victory.

I felt brand, spanking new. I stepped harder, walked taller, and held my head higher. God was creating a women's ministry within me. Afterward, so many women – young and old, saved and not set free, single and married – drew to me, sought prayer, and just wanted to ask "How'd you do it?" I began to see the importance of a life of righteous living. The choices were mine, and there was a harvest for the seed sown, but the hardships and trials were not even about me. God needed to use me to prove who He was, so that His light could shine and draw all those that He was calling.

Many blessings began to pour into my life, quicker than ever. The joy and happiness overshadowed the previous days of drama and tears. About two months after my water, electricity, and phone had all been shut off, after I had no groceries, had been evicted and had given away all of our possessions, I still stood in faith. In fact, I had given my last paycheck to the church- $1000 - in faith, believing that the gift to my church would be a seed sown for good. God didn't let me down.

That very month, only weeks after court, I landed the biggest contract my cleaning company had ever had. Just in passing, I had met a man who bought and sold junk cars, and I had told him about my car history. With the favor of God, he found me a little blue 1989 Toyota Camry that ran well and sold it to me for $300. Once I got that car, I was able to begin marketing my company again, and God restored everything.

I met with a construction company building homes in a development called Habersham in Beaufort. I gave them a proposal, they accepted, and with the help of several friends, we advertised, interviewed, hired and trained ten new, full-time employees, the most people I had ever managed at one time. After only two weeks on the job, my first check from the construction company was over $7000. Every two or three weeks, checks like this continued to roll in as I saw the promise of God. God restored everything that we had lost or that had been taken from us.

In my business, I freely talked about God and the testimony He had given me. Several employees confessed Jesus Christ as their Lord and received the gift of Salvation, as well as visited my church. God continued to bless my business with new commercial and residential accounts almost weekly.

Even my family in St. Louis couldn't deny the blessings. My mom and I became closer as she now often told me how she was proud of me, and she and my aunts playfully began to refer to me as "The Preacher" or an evangelist.

For months, things in my children's and my life seemed to be falling into place. We had moved into a home of our own again, and my business was doing well. I was actively and consistently involved in church and continued to commit to personal time in prayer with God, which had become my core foundation, allowing me to stay focused and live successfully.

For months, Walter was nowhere to be found, as if he had literally dropped off the face of the earth. We never ran into each other, I never inquired about him, and I moved on with my life, completely free of the pain and disappointment I had experienced with him. The days of my emotional freedom were numbered, though, because nearly a year after court, Walter and I began to communicate.

I honestly can't say why or when I felt compelled to make amends with him, but I do recall several key factors. As I matured in my relationship with God, I began to back away from certain things like hip hop, rap, and R&B music, for instance. Several years before, a minister had taught on the negative spiritual effects and influences of certain music. I had chosen to listen only to gospel and Christian music, but after months of doing so, I had gotten a copy of a CD from a popular artist from Walter, late one night after I ran into him at McDonalds.

Everyone was talking about her new CD and I felt compelled to hear it. A year had passed since our court date, and with time and growth, I had moved past and forgotten most of Walter's nasty antics and behavior towards me, forgiving him and remembering him for the friends we used to be. We were not dating, and spoke rarely – only in passing – but we were cordial and had slowly become friends again.

Back at home, I popped the CD into the disc player and immediately became fixed on one particular song, which was, ironically enough, the very song Walter had suggested I listen to.

Over and over, I listened to the artist singing:

"Bells and sirens ringing / she complained of her boyfriend's infidelity
He had been unfaithful and was now flaunting another woman /
She questioned who would put up with this?
She was tired and wanted better / but she couldn't stand
To let another woman be on his arm
She would have the wealth and position / if she chose to walk away
The cars, the house/ If she chose to walk away
She would have what used to be hers / If she chose to walk away
No, she said "I can't let that go."

The artist was singing about how she had left her unworthy, lying, cheating boyfriend who had moved on to start a relationship with "the other woman." With self-respect, dignity, and confidence, she had left him, but now she sang about the way he had quickly forgotten her and was showering the next woman with diamonds, houses, cars, trips, and gifts that used to be hers. She raged about how she wouldn't sit back and let that happen. She felt she had earned the right to those things and that no other woman was going to sit in her place, even if the man had done wrong. To her, it was about principle.

Later that night, I ejected the CD, placed it back in the case, and tossed it in the garbage, realizing that it was nothing I needed to listen to. I went to bed regretting even talking to Walter and wishing that I had never taken the CD and listened to it, but it was too late. Satan had tapped at my door, and I had opened it.

As I lay in bed that night, I kept hearing:

"I'm not sure how to feel / the things that I know, /

I have this intuition / telling me to let you go"

The seed was planted, and for days the words of that song replayed over and over in my head. I found myself contemplating the singers words:

"This other chick has to go. / No other woman can touch his cash flow.
But my heart is so heavy, I know I'm worth more than gold /
Like a movie flick, this story is getting old."

Even more, the memory of Walter's past actions – disrespect, physical and emotional abuse – seemed to completely disappear as I found myself wondering why we had not worked things out.

Walter was dating someone else, and of course he had given her the car that he originally bought for me. After court, it never bothered me, but now it was as if this singer was one of my girls, telling me to not accept that and to get back what was mine. *She* didn't earn that car, and it wasn't intended for *her*.

God knows that I didn't care about Walter, didn't love him anymore, and had no desire to be with him, but I made it my goal to get him back, just so he would take these things away from *her*. Initially, my intention wasn't to hurt her, but I became more aware of her arrogance and her flaunting of *my* things whenever our paths crossed. It fueled a fire, and I didn't care who got burned. I was going to prove that I was the Queen Bee and that I could get him back, even making him drop her like last night's trash.

I got my chance one night while working late at my office. I had walked outside to throw some garbage in a nearby dumpster that sat in a lot separating a small plaza from an auto parts store. As I neared the dumpster, I could see a vehicle, and as I got closer, I realized it was Walter. He had not noticed me yet, and I hesitated before speaking out. Everything within my mind and heart told me to not say a word, to let it go, and to fight to suppress the feelings of anger, envy, and malice I had been feeling.

My mind flashed back to just a few days earlier when I had run into him and his girlfriend, now driving what used to be *my* Lexus. "Her" car and mine were parked side by side in the car wash bays, and when she noticed me, she gave a smug grin and marched around the car to flaunt her ownership of it. In retaliation, I had boldly walked up to Walter to say hello, and he was quick to greet me with an ecstatic hello and a hug.

Now, as I stood in the office parking lot, recalling that moment, I ignored all of the red flags and spoke up to get Walter's attention. We made light conversation, and I told him to come by the office before I left. All the while, my heart and common sense told me this was a bad idea, yet I silenced the thoughts.

Minutes later, I heard a knock at my office door. I was sitting at my desk and before I stood up, and as if someone was literally in the room with me, I clearly heard the voice of God say, "Do not open that door and let him in."

I paused in hesitation, and deep down, I knew that the term "open the door" meant a whole lot more than just the literal sense. It was spiritual, and I was about to open the door to that realm that God had closed just a year ago.

I rationalized God's voice as being "just my own thoughts" and ignored His warnings, more concerned about "winning" and my pride. When Walter came in, he was a bit standoffish, arrogant, and defensive, not exactly sure how to take me. He stood his ground and made it clear that he was over what we had been through, that he had moved on and was happy. To me, because he seemed so unmoved at first, it became my goal to get him back, hook, line and sinker. It was a game to me, and I was determined to win.

By the end of our conversation, Walter was in tears, telling me how sorry he was and how much he regretted everything that he had said and done to me. As he stood there in my office, embracing me, I really didn't feel anything for him at all, as my mind was focused on my plan of action.

It didn't take long for the lines of communication to re-open, and within a month's time, Walter and I were making plans to be together again. Though we were not officially dating yet, he began to spend less time with his girlfriend and more time with me. She knew it, and didn't like it, but couldn't do a thing about it. I knew well that once Walter had made up his mind about being with a woman, nothing else mattered.

Late one evening, just a few weeks before Christmas, I ran into Walter's girlfriend while shopping in the children's section of Wal-Mart. We didn't say a word to one another, but I knew she wanted me to pay close attention to her as she slipped away to browse through the infant and baby aisle. I knew what she was doing, and I patiently waited for the day that Walter would tell me that she was pregnant.

I had insisted that Walter and I be honest and open with one another. He held true to that and had told me everything I wanted to know. If I needed him, he could be found. If I called, he answered. My initial plan to "not care" was quickly falling apart in the face of his newfound honesty.

I never wanted to come out and tell Walter to take the car from his girlfriend because I thought requesting that of him would be too obvious, but I knew that as we continued to rekindle our friendship, I wouldn't *have* to ask. When all was said and done, about two months after that night at my office, Walter had left his pregnant girlfriend, taken the car, and at my request, moved us into a huge, beautiful new house on the water. The house was my Christmas gift that year, my game of chess "checkmate" response.

I told Walter that I didn't want the car, refused to ride in it, and even told him to let the other woman have it. I wanted a new one, and less than a month later, he took me, on the spur of the moment, to purchase a bigger, newer, white Lexus LS. At least this time I had sense enough to keep his name off my car's title, bill of sale, and insurance policy.

I kept the news of Walter and my reuniting to myself because it was never my plan to take it as far as it had gone. Now living together, we were inseparable. Our relationship seemed stronger, more stable, and better than ever. All the things he had been in the past were no more. He was faithful, honest, compassionate, and committed. He worked hard to be good to the children and me, and there was nothing I asked for that he wouldn't get me.

At this point, we began discussing marriage, so I knew I had to let friends and family know. All of them were shocked, angry, and concerned. They couldn't understand it, didn't agree with it, and refused to believe it, but over time they accepted it, because it was what I wanted. I realized how he had changed and even defended him against their harsh but properly founded criticism and judgment. I used God as a crutch, saying how He was preparing Walter to be a good husband, though I knew deep down that God had nothing to do with this.

Still, even after seeking counsel from my pastor and his wife, who spoke openly with me about the fact that I was exemplifying low self-esteem by wanting this relationship and didn't realize that I deserved better, without thinking, I said yes to Walter's marriage proposal on

Valentine’s Day 2006.

YOUR JOURNAL

Pride is defined as a high or inordinate opinion of one's own dignity, importance, merit or superiority, and it can be viewed with both positive and negative connotations. When we allow pride to consume our relationships, thoughts, and actions, the outcome is rarely ever positive. In what areas have you allowed pride to cause you to accept less than the best? In what areas has pride caused you to stop being and giving your best to others?

CHAPTER EIGHTEEN

In this freedom Christ has made us free and completely liberated us; stand fast then, and do not be hampered and held ensnared and submit again to a yoke of slavery which you have once put off.

– Galatians 5:1

As elated as I attempted to appear and convince myself to be, when Walter proposed, my feelings weren't genuine. I wanted to rebuild our lives together, from the earlier days, before things went bad, but that life was a lie. I had initiated a relationship with Walter purely to deceive and hurt all those who had hurt me; however, along the way, I had never thought of an exit plan.

For weeks after he proposed, I constantly thought about how wrong things were turning out to be, but I felt so trapped by my commitment that I continued to plan the wedding, shopping for a dress, and playing house as if nothing were wrong.

I had not considered my children in my selfish decision-making. My son, who at four years old was too young to know otherwise, loved Walter, who had been the only male figure he had ever really had in his life.

Things with my daughter were different. Nikole was 10 years old and had made it clear that she didn't want us to live with Walter. I tried to convince her that he was different now, that he wasn't going to be mean or hurt me. She reluctantly warmed up to the idea as he "bought" his way back into her heart, showering her and Elijah with toys, clothes, money, and anything they desired

Though I seemed able to deny a lot, I couldn't ignore the fact that Walter and I were not spiritually equal. As memories of our past began to resurface, I snapped back into reality. I wanted to end the relationship – the engagement at least – but I was fearful that my children and I would lose everything and that he would take it all from us again. Business had stopped completely – I had lost the contract I had been awarded, due to failed inspections – so I was now financially dependent on Walter. He had complete control, and I had nothing.

My devious plan had backfired, and I now found myself as the one without control. I had no sense of security or trust. I questioned everything Walter did, every place he went, and every phone call he made. We began to argue all the time, and he would come home later and later, frustrated and angry with me, and caring less and less about my feelings. I resented him – hated him even – as I began to think more of what he had done to me in the past.

I was angry with myself for having taken Walter back, yet I stayed because I was too ashamed to talk to my friends about the stupid mistakes I had made. Besides, I had nowhere to go. I had completely isolated myself from my church and felt way too condemned to go back, though I longed to be there.

The only consolation I could find was to mask my pain with alcohol and cigarettes. Walter hated both drinking and smoking, so I hid them from him but chain-smoked relentlessly on nights after we would fight and on days when he wouldn't come home. Sometimes, I would just get in my car and ride for an hour or so, smoking half a pack of Newport 100s to calm my nerves and ease my mind.

One night, Walter and I got into such a huge fight about him coming home so late, that as he ran across the room at me, I just stood in the door defiantly, without flinching, waiting for his blow to come. "I don't care anymore," I thought. "I'm tired of all of this."

He stopped his punch in mid-air, and instead of reaching out to hit or grab me, he lifted his foot to kick me in the face. He was wearing steel-toed Timberland construction boots, and it had to be God's mercy that stopped him, because with his foot less than an inch from my face, he froze, slowly dropped his foot, and walked out of the room. His foot had been so close that I could have stuck my tongue out and licked the bottom of his boot.

Then he came back and proceeded to curse me out, shouting profanities loudly, trying to wake the children. He walked toward their room, yelling that he didn't care if he woke them. Fearful for them, I began to pack our suitcases and told Walter that I would leave, which only upset him more. He bellowed that I wasn't going to leave him, only to turn around, snatch my suitcases, and throw them out the door, so far that they landed in the neighbor's driveway. He then began yelling at me to "Get out!"

The kids and I stayed in a hotel that night, and even though I eventually went back, it was only to pack up more of our things. We went to stay with a friend in Charlotte, North Carolina for about a week. I didn't tell Walter where I was, nor did I answer his calls for days.

I didn't want to go back, but I had grown so insecure and become so dependent on him that I felt as if I literally had nothing without him.

After the week in Charlotte, as we walked back through the front door that we had been thrown out of, I was scared of Walter's reaction. Though he was rarely home during the day, I noticed that his car was in the driveway. When he heard me come in, he stepped into the foyer and hugged me with tears in his eyes.

The "break up to make up" cycle wasn't over yet. Months passed as Walter and I struggled to deal with one another and make the relationship work. Then late one night, after one of our usual arguments about his failure to come home, I went to the emergency room for chest pain. I was having problems breathing and experiencing sharp pains. Walter had been gone all day, and I now needed him but couldn't reach him on his cell phone. I called over and over again until finally he answered, agitated that I had kept calling. After telling him what was going on, he told me that he was busy. He said he'd try to come to the emergency room, but he never did, nor did he even call later to see if I was okay. Fortunately, I wasn't having a heart attack; however, for the first time in my life, I was told that I was suffering from stress, panic attacks, and anxiety.

Later that week, not wanting Walter to hear my conversation, I snuck outside to call my mom. She was the only person I felt I could reach out to talk to, in the hope that she would give me the motherly advice I was seeking. I didn't tell her everything that was going on, just that I was unhappy and didn't want to marry Walter. I told her that I felt guilty for even getting back with him, which had ruined both our lives. I said that I felt obligated to marry him, since the wedding was only a month away.

My mom reassured me that no one would be upset or disappointed if the wedding didn't happen. If I wasn't happy, she said that she would support my decision and encouraged me not to go through with it. She said she had known something was wrong because when she and I spoke, I was no longer "myself," and she always heard it in my voice.

After that night, Walter and I mutually agreed to postpone the wedding but remain engaged and live together. Though I had taken that one step forward, my life felt as if it kept spiraling downward. Walter continued to dominate my world. I had completely withdrawn from church fellowship and association; I was depressed and withdrawn from my friends. Walter seemed to always be working and never home. When he was, he always came in late and would sleep on the couch. I couldn't sleep when he wasn't home, as I obsessed about who he was with and where he was. Of course, I assumed that he was seeing another woman, and questioned both myself and him as to why he was even in the relationship with me. Each time he denied seeing other women, he seemed to want to comfort me, but then he would always ruin it by ending with comments that insinuated that he should cheat in order to find relief from my nagging and complaining.

I continued to drink and smoke until I was so numb that my days just ran together. With each new argument, which was pretty much a day to day routine, Walter became meaner and nastier than before. I hated him, and I hated myself even more for staying.

I was home alone one day, flipping through TV channels, and I stopped to watch a show called "Snapped." It was based on true stories in which ordinary women felt pushed to the point of no return and "snapped," murdering their husbands or lovers. I chuckled as I watched, thinking how I could relate to the term "snapped." I felt like I was definitely in the "hell hath no fury like a woman scorned" category.

Yet, as detached from God as I felt, I heard His small, still voice gently tell me to not watch the show. But I overrode that order, and became transfixed on the program daily. I tuned in so often that Walter noticed, commenting that I was "always" watching it. Without thought, and using words that didn't seem to be mine, I calmly replied, "Yes, I do, because these women on this show got caught. I'm taking notes so that I don't."

For the first time since I had known him, Walter seemed unsure of my stability and sanity as he nervously giggled when I pulled my eyes off the TV to meet his. I gave him a blank stare, empty of emotion, blinked, and then turned my gaze back to the TV as he left the room. The moment I said those words, it was as if every dark, demonic power attempting to control me was released. I had never had such thoughts, nor knew they even existed, but a seed had been planted in me, and its roots were taking hold.

"What if I killed him?" I wondered. "He deserves it, doesn't he? Could I get away with it?" I recalled that there was an insurance policy on his life that I would benefit from.

Though I was able to dismiss these thoughts, I found myself occasionally testing his strength and health, by intentionally cooking him expired meat or sour food. Though I believed I wasn't consciously trying to kill him or make him sick, I also didn't hesitate whenever it occurred to me to "test" him. I even remember calling a girlfriend of mine to ask her if she knew what types of food would give a person food poisoning. She assumed that I only wanted a remedy to the problem because I claimed Walter had eaten some freezer-burned fish.

One day in mid-summer, I was leaving the house as Walter was just getting in from one of his late nights out. It was about seven or eight o'clock in the morning, and I was headed out to handle a cleaning job for a client. When I asked him where he had been, he angrily began cussing me out, calling me "stupid," which was the most polite word that came out of his mouth. He said that we didn't have any kind of relationship if he had to answer to me about his whereabouts all of the time, and that he wasn't going to continue to live his life with me like this if I didn't change.

The kids were asleep, and I normally left them with him whenever I went to work this early, but as Walter went into our bedroom to sleep, I quietly dressed them. I had not planned on taking them, but within me, satan was whispering ideas about how I could take Walter's life. I calmly walked toward the front door, and considered how simple it would be to turn the thermostat so high that he would have a stroke in his sleep.

I backed out of the driveway, imagining the relief I would feel, if when my children and I returned home, I found him dead in our bed, appearing to be sleep.

God's grace and mercy didn't allow the enemy to use me to take Walter's life, but it wasn't the last time I ever thought about it. Though I had never thought of taking my own life, I had become so fearfully complacent in the relationship that I believed the only way out was for one of us to die.

YOUR JOURNAL

Have you ever worn a garment that was too small, tight and constricting? Recall the feeling of relief you had when you were finally able to remove it and be free of its uncomfortable restraint. Being in an unhealthy relationship or a dead-end friendship can feel the same way. The Bible tells us to not be unequally yoked in bondage to things or people who are not like-minded to us. Write about those things or people in your life and why you feel the strain of them. Ask God to remove you from this bondage and help you not to return to it.

CHAPTER NINETEEN

For no temptation has overtaken you and laid hold on you that is not common to man. But God is faithful, and He can be trusted not to let you be tempted and tried beyond your ability and strength of resistance and power to endure, but with the temptation He will always provide the way out, that you may be capable and strong and powerful to bear up under it patiently.

– 1 Corinthians 10:13

For close to nine months, Walter and I stayed in this unhealthy relationship, even moving into a bigger, more elaborate home than the first and adding a new car to the three we already owned. All of Walter's apologies took the form of gifts. He had so much cash that at times I wondered if he was dabbling in drug trafficking again. His response was always "No," and unless he was cunning about how he did things, I never saw any evidence that he was.

Walter sought a fictitious lifestyle, in which money, cars, houses and a pretty girl were the center of his life. I think that he painted this ideal image of who we were supposed to be and how we were supposed to act, and his money allowed him to keep control of all of that. I suppose to him, I was an arm candy girlfriend: smart, beautiful, young, independent, and a "good girl" worth marrying.

Yet I didn't feel like I was any of those things anymore. Of my own will, I had allowed this man to break my spirit. I felt ugly, overweight, stupid, old, worthless and insecure, yet I was barely 30 years old, a size 9, a business owner since the age of 23, and rarely went anywhere without getting a look or positive compliment from the opposite sex.

The roller coaster quality of our relationship intensified with constant arguments that inevitably resulted in days of us not speaking to each other and nights of Walter sleeping in the guest house or not coming home at all. I slipped into a deeper depression, and for weeks, I never left the house.

Walter would take the children to and from school while I stayed home in bed. I didn't care about anything and had just quit trying. I had accepted my fate and believed that I was either going to kill or be killed. I hated Walter and I wanted out of the relationship so badly, but I no longer had the strength to leave. I truly felt worthless and disabled at the thought of my life with or without him.

If it were not for my children, I don't believe I would have snapped back into existence. I finally realized that for their sake, I couldn't give up or let them down. Where would they go without a mother? Who would take care of them? Would they even be able to stay together? Those questions and the terrible answers gripped me with a fear like I had never felt in my life. The only thing worse than me dying would have been leaving my two children alone in a world without the genuine, compassionate care of their mother.

God finally prompted me and gave me the strength to begin to communicate with Him again. For a year, I had dangerously chosen to back away from God and had intentionally chosen sin and Walter over Him. Yet, faithful as always, God never left me. He never removed His grace, mercy, and protection from me. I turned my back on Him, but when I turned around, He was still right there, beckoning me with open arms.

I began reading my Bible and praying again. Walter was never home, so he didn't notice, but as I began to seek God more, my sleepless nights ended. I no longer cared when and whether or not Walter came home. I began to actually prefer that he didn't. My tears over Walter turned into praise and worship unto God.

Later, when Walter attempted to reconcile with me and to be home and in bed as he should have always done, I began sleeping upstairs with my kids. I no longer desired him, and knew that we couldn't sleep together. As the days went on, I knew our living together had to end.

One day, while the children were at school, Walter and I got into an argument. I really don't recall what it was about, but he called the police on me. I had not done anything crazy or outlandish, but he was making a power move, just as a parent might call a child's bluff by threatening to call the cops.

Walter knew how terribly afraid I was of going back to jail, and we both knew that he was capable of fabricating a story. Like a child, I begged and pleaded with him to not call the police. I cried so hard that I shook, terrified that I would get locked up and no one would be there to pick up my kids from school, which would get the Department of Social Services involved. However, as his character repeatedly proved, he didn't care about that. He said that if DSS took my kids away when I didn't show up for them, it wasn't his problem.

We were upstairs in the guest house, and as he spoke to the 911 operator, I ran downstairs and into the main house. I grabbed my car keys, but then realized his car was blocking mine in. I knew better than to take his car; he would just lie and report it stolen. By now, the police would be on their way, and though I had done nothing, I panicked at the thought of them arresting me and my kids being left alone. I grabbed my cell phone and darted out the front door, running across our neighbor's back lawn into some nearby woods.

I had no clue where I was going, but I needed to get away and hide. I felt like a fugitive as my adrenaline-fueled heart pounded in my chest. In the woods, I ran under, around, and over brush, ripping my clothes on snares and bruising my skin on branches.

I came to a swamp area and turned to look back, certain that I was being chased. I wanted to stop – fearful of running through the alligator-filled marsh – but I couldn't. "What will happen to my children if the police catch me?" I worried. I held my breath and ran as fast as I could, praying that there were no deep drop offs or sink holes in the water.

"I'm going to die, right here, eaten alive by alligators," I thought, as I splashed my way across the muddy water. On the other side of the marsh, I ran through another wooded area and ended up at the back of a country club golf course. I looked like a wild mess as I calmed down and jogged across the course.

I found a cul de sac to hide in and sat there for at least an hour, trying to figure out what to do. I managed to call a friend, and though I didn't tell her what had happened, I calmly asked her to pick up my kids from school for me. Once I knew that they were safe and secure, I realized that I had to go back home. I left my place of safety and, full of dread, walked back to the house.

Walter was still there, alone and supposedly worried about me. He said a neighbor had seen me run into the woods, and even though he had called the police, he claimed that he had done it merely to avoid a dangerous outcome to our argument. To me, that sounded like he was just trying to cover his guilty tracks. I knew then that it was time to get out of this relationship for good.

My opportunity came, unexpectedly, about a week later. It was early morning, and the children didn't have school. I ran out to the grocery store, and when I came back, Walter was getting dressed to leave for work. Everything he said and did irritated me, and I was impatient with him all morning. My actions finally triggered a reaction in him and he began cussing me out and calling me all kinds of names, so I came right back at him, telling him how much I hated him. My defiance angered him further, and he stopped ironing his shirt and began walking threateningly towards me, yelling and cussing as he came closer, stopping halfway as my children came running downstairs.

Nikole, now 10, and Elijah, 4, both stared at Walter with wide, wild eyes as he continued to curse at us all. My body went numb, and I couldn't hear anything. I felt as if God took me out of my body to truly look at the scene. Walter's face was angry and contorted, ready to hurt me. When I looked at my daughter, I saw fear, anguish, and tears. When I looked at my son, he yelled "Yeah, get him, get him!" to me.

"What are you teaching your children?" I heard God say. "That terrifying women is okay? That it's alright for men to feel empowered by abusing and disrespecting women?"

As these words entered my mind, all sound and motion came rushing back, and before Walter could come any closer, I grabbed my kids and keys and rushed out the front door. We were all in our pajamas and had no shoes on our feet. I never looked back to see if Walter was following us, but I knew that I wasn't going to turn back. My heart was pounding as I shoved my children into the car and sped off. I was scared because of the emotional scene that we had just left, but at the same time I felt relieved to be free of Walter and that house.

I didn't know where I was going or who to call. I drove to the bank and sat in the parking lot, contemplating whether or not to empty our joint account and leave. After about a half hour, I convinced myself to just take all the money and drive to my parents' house, 14 hours away, in St. Louis.

I didn't plan on staying forever; I just needed to get away and think, but hours into driving, I realized that I couldn't ever go back to Walter. He was going to be angry that I had left him and even angrier that I had taken all the money.

In St. Louis, I was very vague and evasive with my parents about what happened. But I told them that I had left Walter and wanted to come home. A day later, I left my kids with my mom, while two of my male cousins, an uncle, and I drove back to South Carolina to pack up my belongings. I took my family for help and protection, but I can't say that I objected when they suggested that they "whoop Walter's butt." Honestly, I had flickering thoughts of my own about them tying him up and tossing him in the closet while we packed the entire house. Better yet, throwing him in the back of the moving truck and letting him loose somewhere in the backwoods of Tennessee. Needless to say, and thank God, we kept our composure and didn't carry out any of these fantasies.

Walter, on the other hand, was irate about my leaving. Though I had done nothing but begin to pack, he called the police to attempt to have me arrested for packing things that were mine but that he claimed were his. He disputed my right to practically everything I picked up to pack, including the children's bedroom furniture, most of which I had paid for. Of course, the police had no grounds to arrest me and could only mediate between the two of us; however, things turned so petty that I gave up and took only clothing, shoes and toys.

As a further insult, Walter called and asked his friend Kevin to come over, in some attempt, I suppose, to convince me to stay. Kevin brought his girlfriend with him, and she was now freely walking through the house "oohing" and "ahhing" over it while she was on the phone with one of her girlfriends. She whispered that I was leaving Walter, and she would introduce her friend to him. Normally, I would have slapped the phone out of her hand and the taste out of her mouth, but I didn't even care. I was so over it all and just ready to have my life back.

That day, October 17, 2007, was the day I walked out of Walter's life forever, never to look back ever again. We had to jump through some hoops to get the children transferred and enrolled in school in Missouri, but we finally settled in, and I began to adjust to our new life. However, as much as I tried, it just wasn't what I wanted it to be.

I worked a regular 9:00 to 5:00 work week, at Express Personnel, a local agency that offered daily work to the temporarily unemployed. I went to church on Sundays and Wednesdays, paying into the offering and keeping a savings account, yet I just couldn't get ahead. My children stayed sick constantly and seemed to alternate trips to the emergency room with each other. There was never enough money for anything, and living in my parents' basement, sharing a bed with my two children, wasn't working at all. My parents were patient and gracious to receive us, but even when I enrolled in some college courses, it didn't help. I was out of God's will and plan, and the devil was prowling.

One day, my son's teacher questioned me after Elijah had told her, "Daddy pushed Mommy into a wall." Ashamed and embarrassed, I quickly explained that my former fiancé and I were no longer involved. I was now working as an administrative assistant, which for me, compared to owning and managing my own business, was a dead end job. Though I attended a local faith-filled church that taught from the

Bible, I sincerely missed my home church, Life House Church, back in Beaufort, South Carolina.

In St. Louis, I attended the Greater Pentecostal Church, yet during most services I realized that I already knew much of the message that was being taught. Not learning anything new made me feel as if my spiritual growth was also at a standstill.

I read and I prayed, but day in and day out, I just existed, seeming to have no purpose in my life. I felt defeated, and my battle with depression began again, but this time, God wouldn't allow it.

YOUR JOURNAL

Many times we allow ourselves – even talk ourselves into or out of – the very opposite of what we need most. Quick thought or fleeting actions can be the very thing to literally save our lives. God is always talking, and we need to position ourselves to always be listening. When He speaks, he doesn't change His mind. God promised to give us a way to escape everything we could possibly go through, including situations in which we selfishly placed ourselves. Write to God and tell Him about the situation you are in now, asking Him to show you His way of escape.

CHAPTER TWENTY

If my people, who are called by My name, shall humble themselves, pray, seek, crave, and require of necessity My face and turn from their wicked ways, then will I hear from heaven, forgive their sin, and heal their land.
– 2 Chronicles 7:14

One night, after months of "just living" and not committing to or truly seeking God, I was in the basement, deeply asleep. I suddenly sat up and began to pray intensely in the Spirit. It felt as if it were beyond my control as I prayed, tears streaming from my eyes. I bent forward and bowed to my knees in the middle of the bed as fear gripped me: not terror but a feeling of deep *reverence*. I felt a presence in the room as I prayed harder and louder until my fear turned into complete and total peace.

I repented for backing away from God, and He began to speak to me about His will for my life. He reminded me of a message that one of the ministers at my church in South Carolina had taught. He referred to me as a plant rooted in the right, healthy soil where it would thrive and grow versus that same plant being uprooted and planted in foreign soil in a climate and environment not conducive to its growth and health, which would die. I wasn't thriving and prospering in St. Louis because I was that uprooted plant, now dying.

After almost six months in St. Louis, it was time to leave and go back to Beaufort. I would start fresh and reconnect with my good soil, Life House Church. The very first day back in South Carolina, I ran into Walter at a local shopping plaza. He looked stunned to see me back in town, but I just cordially waved and continued on without stopping to speak.

A friend had said that the children and I could move in with her until I got on my feet; however, this arrangement fell through as I realized my initial suggestion to pay more than half the rent wasn't wise, as I hadn't yet found a job and was left with no finances for anything else. Not even a week later, though, I was hired as a front office administrative assistant for a local furniture and interior design company. Obtaining a job helped to prepare the children and me to move into our own place.

While out driving one Sunday after church, I came across a house for rent and called the realtor, Julia, for details. I didn't know it at the time, but this realtor would turn out to be a godsend and true, life-long friend to my children and me.

After about a month or so of showing me potential homes, she found us a small, fully furnished house with three bedrooms, one bath, and all the dishes, linens, and anything else we could possibly need to live. Utilities were included in the rent, and the furnished home was ideal for us because I no longer had any household items. The children and I barely even had any clothing or shoes left because most of it was left behind in St. Louis as we had packed only what could fit in my car for our move back.

Back in Beaufort, back in my church, working, and finally in a home of our own, things seemed to be looking up after years of drama, stress, abuse, and struggle. My number one priority was to stay focused on God and create a stable, peaceful, happy home for my children and me. I made a solemn vow to myself and to God that He was all I needed, and that until He Himself sent me a husband, I had no desire to date or to seek a relationship on my own. I had had enough, and my children had seen and been dragged through enough, as well.

Though I was renting, I wanted to purchase a home to truly call our own. With my realtor's help, I completed a loan application to begin the process. I wanted a place that no man could take from us. While I was renting, I managed to make my payments in full and on time, but I was staying in a fully furnished vacation rental property. Though the landlord had decreased the rent by nearly $500 a month, $375 per week soon turned out to be too much to handle, as it was exactly how much I was making per week at my job. There was nothing left after I paid rent each week. Gas, food, and other expenses ate away at my savings.

I didn't know what I was going to do, but I knew that I couldn't stay there much longer. The rental was supposed to be short-term, to allow my realtor friend and me time to get my loan approved and find a house. However, new obstacles presented themselves daily, which prolonged the application process. Julia helped in any way she could. She and her husband, Richard, even offered to open their home to us when I told her that I needed to move out of the rental because I could no longer afford it.

To make matters worse, the business I worked for began to have financial problems, and several times the employees' pay was either delayed or we were paid short of what we were owed. For months, I had worked so hard to clean up my credit, pay off debt, and obtain an acceptable credit score to be approved for home ownership, and it was quickly slipping from my grasp because I wasn't being paid enough or on time.

I was still driving the second Lexus Walter had gotten me but decided that I should sell it for the extra cash. The car was the final trace of him left in my life, and we desperately needed money, so I sold it without hesitation or regret.

I had another "run around" vehicle – a rusty gray Chevy with fading and chipped paint and a ripped and hanging headliner – that I had left behind with a friend when I initially left for St. Louis. It was such a "lemon" of a car, but I didn't care about the downgrade. I had had enough of the false, glitzy and worldly wealth that the devil had tempted me with in my time with Walter. As a child of God, the daughter of a King, I knew that wealth and prosperity would be inevitable, but I now only wanted it God's way: No more false prosperity. I would definitely wait for the "real."

Julia, Richard, and their son, Aaron, who was the same age as Elijah, lived in a huge house in a beautiful neighborhood right on the river. Aaron, who was the only child, had three rooms of his own on most of the second floor, so the family offered that level of their home to my children and me. They opened their home and hearts to us, even trusting us to be left at home alone when they were out, no questions asked.

I had chosen not to tell friends, church, or family what I was going through, so no one but Julia knew. As hospitable and welcoming as they were, I felt uncomfortable living and eating with complete strangers. I am still not sure if it was my pride or truly feeling like I was imposing, but I told Julia that I felt as if my children and I needed a place of our own.

Julia let me know that she owned some land and horse stables that had a barn and tack room. With no money, but not feeling comfortable enough to continue to stay on in Julia's home, I accepted her offer to live rent-free in the tack room of the barn. It was a small open room, furnished with a dining table, a TV, and a sofa. There was a small bathroom with a sink and shower attached. The barn held a washer, dryer, exterior sink, and a refrigerator. Outside the tack room, a mid-size trailer designed for transporting horses had a cabin up front with a bed. This is where my children and I would sleep at night.

This way of living was totally different from anything I had ever experienced, but I felt I had no other choice. I chose to keep quiet about our circumstances, not out of shame or embarrassment, but because I didn't want the pity, remarks, or comments of others. I needed to remain focused and keep my trust in God. My current situation was the result of choices and decisions that *I* had made, the consequences of my own actions, the harvest of seeds sown.

I never thought once to question or resent God. Like many times before, I knew that He was there for me. He was watching my faith, and I could believe and trust in Him because He already knew the outcome. I just needed to trust Him, and in fact I truly did.

As a mother, some days were especially hard, as we were literally living in a barn. My mornings consisted of feeding my kids, then walking only steps away to feed the two horses in the stalls near the tack room. I knew my kids were suffering because of my actions, and I cried a lot, particularly on rainy days when the roof leaked and damaged what few shoes I had left. On hot days, the sweltering heat drove ants and spiders into the dark coolness of the tack room. A water moccasin found its way into the bathroom, and we kept finding it coiled and sleeping in the toilet until Julia finally smashed and killed it for me.

Yes, some days were definitely harder than others, but throughout it all, I cried out only to God. I prayed consistently, and honestly, we were happy. My children loved living on a farm and being around the horses and dogs. There was a huge open field for them to play in, and all they truly cared about was that we were together, back in South Carolina among friends and church family, and away from Walter. Their joy and happiness kept me grounded and at peace.

We continued our lives as normally as we could and attended school and church without ever showing that we were pretty much homeless. I did, however, tell my children to keep quiet about how we lived, for fear they would be taken by their fathers or by child welfare. Shortly after moving into the barn, I started the application process for Section 8 government housing assistance.

We lived in the tack room for about two months before my daughter's godmother found out and invited us to live with her. Her home didn't have room for all three of us, so we converted the garage into a livable space and stayed there for over a month until my housing approval finally came, and we moved into a home with affordable rent.

During this process, my income at my job continued to be in limbo.

The corporation I worked for was near bankruptcy but had not shut down. We had not been paid properly or on time in weeks, and my child support was all the income I had, yet I still trusted God.

Then, one Sunday during service, my pastor began to speak prophetically with the congregation about each of our futures and finances. As I stood to my feet to raise my hands and praise God, my pastor said, “God says, the struggle is over!”

At that point, everything in me just broke. I couldn’t control the hot tears that turned into open sobs as I began to praise God. I *knew* that through the pastor, God was talking directly to me, and it wasn’t much longer before my blessing came through.

The only child support I received was $450 a month for my daughter from her father. My son’s father, Warren, had not paid in years and had managed to avoid all of my and the state’s attempts to collect back pay. Only by an act of God had Warren contacted me to suggest that we go together to Family Court and reinstate his child support payments. Warren kept his word, and though he was now living out of South Carolina, he drove there for court, and without argument signed all documentation to willingly pay child support.

In addition, Warren was now receiving social security benefits because he had an illness called sarcoidosis, which attacks and deteriorates the body's vital organs. He had chosen to make our son a beneficiary, so during the social security application process, we were told that Elijah should receive back pay for the three years his father had been collecting SSI. However, due to Warren listing his other children who were born after Elijah as beneficiaries, I was told that the back pay would be split among them all, and Elijah would be likely to receive only $82 a month from SSI.

But I continued to believe that God had deemed our "struggle over." A couple of weeks after filing, I called the SSI office from work to check on the status of the deposit. I pulled up my bank account online just as the SSI clerk told me that the deposit had been made. My account had been overdrawn for days, and was about to be closed by the bank. I had been hoping that the $82 deposit would at least put a dent in the overdrawn balance of - $549.32 and show some activity on the account.

My eyes flew open wide and my hands shook as I stared at my computer screen: the deposit was for nearly $9,000, every penny Elijah was owed for the years of SSI back pay. I began weeping and praising

God, and the SSI clerk on the phone joined in. My co-workers came running to see if I was okay, and after I explained what had happened, they all smiled and cried with me. God had answered my prayers and was laying the foundation for my life renewed in Him.

For the next year, my life only got better. I continued to draw closer to God. In the past, I had connected quickly and deeply with people whom I thought I knew and could trust, but I was wrong. Now I learned from, listened to, and observed my surroundings closely, and God began to transform me into what He had called me to be all along. I endured minor obstacles and tests, but the lessons and growth were major. Daily life situations offered me valuable instruction in faith, forgiveness, friendship, and trust.

During the summer of 2009, Nikole complained of stomach pain and nausea but later said it had subsided. A few days later, however, when we were leaving Sunday service, she was doubled over and in tears from an agonizing pain in her stomach. I took her home to rest, assuming, since she was 11 years old, the "crampy" feeling was the onset of her menstrual cycle.

I prayed with her, laid her on the couch, and went into the kitchen to get her some Tylenol. As I opened the cabinet and reached for the bottle, I simply heard the word "No." I hesitated with my hand actually resting on the bottle and thought about what I had heard. My mind told me that she needed the medication for the pain and slight fever she was running, yet I also felt that the "No" was God speaking to me. I left the bottle in the cabinet and went to check on her. She slept for hours but woke up groggy, had a higher temperature, and was still in pain.

I prayed, asking God what was going on, and He responded, "It's her appendix." Fear gripped me, and as I rushed to my computer, the research of her symptoms confirmed the signs of appendicitis. I quickly dressed her, and at the emergency room, doctors determined she did in fact need emergency surgery to remove her infected appendix.

The doctor asked me if I had given her anything and was relieved to hear that I had not given her any anti-inflammatory medicine such as Tylenol because it could have actually sped up the agitation of the appendix and caused it to rupture and burst, resulting in death. I now knew why God told me "No" when I had reached for the Tylenol.

The surgery was a success, and she spent a few days in the hospital healing. This incident furthered our faith and increased our trust in God.

As days turned into weeks, and the week's months, then years, my children and I grew closer, stronger and happier. Life became more stable and permanent as God continued to heal the wounds and scars of the past, yet diligently and faithfully structuring our future for the better.

YOUR JOURNAL

Sometimes, all it takes is realizing that we have a responsibility for certain things that happen to us. Not accepting responsibility can be the obstacle that hinders growth within us. Many people and many things can cause us pain and affliction, but there are times that we can do just the same to ourselves. Today, take a look within and be honest with yourself about how, why, and when you arrived at the place where you are now.

EPILOGUE

Fear not, there is nothing to fear, for I am with you;
do not look around you in terror and be dismayed, for I am your God.
I will strengthen you and harden you to difficulties,
yes, I will help you; yes I will hold you up and retain you with
My victorious right hand of righteousness and justice

– Isaiah 41:10

Today, ironically enough, my parents are in town visiting the children and me. We are on our way to Florida for a vacation at a resort. It's been a whole month since I last wrote, but today, on my way out the door, I felt led by God to bring my journal along and write. Honestly, I hesitated because the last thing I want at this time is for one of my parents to come across this journal and read it. Which brings me to my next thought: when and how do I tell them I am writing a book? For now, all I can say is that I thank God for being able to place my cares in His hands. It is He who gave me direction about writing this book, so it is in Him that I place my trust to work the details out within my family.

As I am now sitting in the backseat, my children beside me, my dad driving, and my mom in the passenger seat, I am faced with the truth of God's reality. I am a new creation. A smile is on my face as I can freely write of my past trials, tribulations, obstacles, anguish, and pain without batting an eye or dropping a tear. It's all gone, and I have no anger or hatred, no hurt, and no regrets. I have Jesus and as I love Him, I love them. Only Jesus could and would allow me to sit in complete and total peace right in the midst of those who had once planned my fall. I am full of love, ready and willing to stand on the word of God, attentive to pray for their souls.

God is so good. Both my children - Nikole, now 15, and Elijah, now 9 – have confessed Christ as their Lord and savior, and both my mother and father have received salvation.

My mother's prayer for salvation came several years ago during a conversation between us about the difference between baptism and salvation. For years, after I had come into the knowledge, I attempted to explain the difference between the two of them to my mother. Our conversations had always ended with my frustration over her insisting that she was saved because of her water baptism. She would pull her "seniority card" on me every time and refuse to listen to me. In her eyes, I was just her child who knew nothing compared to all the years she had grown up and attended church.

This particular conversation took place only a day after an argument in which I had vowed to myself to never have anything else to do with my family. However, I found myself picking up the phone to call my mother. That morning, during my prayer and devotional time, God had spoken to me and told me to call her. He had made it clear that it wasn't His will for me to just disconnect from my family so abruptly. I am so grateful for God's guidance that morning, because during that phone call, my mother chose to listen to me explain salvation, and we ended our conversation with a prayer and her accepting Jesus Christ.

It is now 2012, five years since we came back to South Carolina after I finally ended my relationship with Walter and we lost everything we had. God has restored so much for my children and me. I left Walter in 2007 and have been happily single ever since. God has allowed me this time to be strengthened in Him, to fall in love with Him, and we have enjoyed a stable, happy home life ever since. For the past five years, I finally ended the long pattern of having men drop in and out of my life. God has continued to propel me upward in every way.

From mid-2008 to 2010, I re-established my cleaning company, obtaining many commercial and residential accounts as well as employing several individuals to work for me. The cleaning company was fine, but after 10 years of hard labor, I was ready for a change. In March 2010, I went to school to enter the beauty industry, earning my certification in three different trades and became a permanent cosmetic professional and beauty consultant, specializing in semi-permanent eyelash extension enhancement and eyebrow threading.

After getting my certification, I rented and renovated a small storefront and dubbed my business a "beauty boutique." It is the only one of its kind in the area, offering specialty beauty enhancement services to women. In less than a year, I had seen and serviced close to 500 clients, and my business is still growing. My beauty boutique has afforded me a new standard of living, and I have been featured in several publications, websites, blogs, and newspaper articles about my business and the uniqueness of the services it offers. I have also obtained a position as a beauty columnist for the local newspaper and was selected by an international cosmetic and skin care line to be the spokesperson for their televised ad campaign and commercials.

This year, so far, I have hired and trained two assistants to help me in the expansion of my second location, and with the growth and popularity of my services, I became a national educator, traveling throughout the East Coast with my children, teaching and training other beauty industry professionals.

New doors are opening, as I accomplished graduating college in December 2012 and have obtained my cosmetology license with a diploma in Applied Sciences to further enhance my business. Upon starting school in May 2011, I managed to run an expanding business full time, successfully parent my two beautiful children, and maintain a 4.0 GPA, making the Dean's and President's lists every semester.

As a faithful and dedicated member of Life House Church, I continue to attend services regularly and have since been promoted to a leadership auxiliary, overseeing and encouraging the Women's Fellowship.

My future goals are to open spas throughout the United States and to launch my own beauty school and distributorship. The school will offer training and certification to equip others with the opportunity to own a franchise of my beauty boutique. I know what it is to have seen struggle as a young mother and as a woman. God's presence was my strength and by His will I plan to offer programs for others to be given the same opportunities that I have had.

Further personal goals are to begin motivational speaking engagements to empower women and young girls with the knowledge they need to succeed and the support they deserve to overcome their lives' obstacles.

In all of this, I give God all of the recognition and glory. None of this was or ever will be *my* doing. The women's ministry within me has taken on the form and purpose of God. I see many, many women in my boutique, and we all have a story. I don't for one minute resent or regret one thing about my past because God has truly equipped me with the experience and knowledge, compassion and understanding to relate to many of these women. I have gone through the fire without being burned, and because of God's grace, mercy, and power, I have emerged without even the smell of smoke lingering. My words to every woman are: with God, *you* can, too.

I have laughed, cried, embraced, and prayed with many of my clients, some of whom have become close friends, ranging in age from their mid-20s to late 60s. Hurt and pain know no age, and sorrow has no boundaries. Abuse and neglect are colorblind, yet as women, we are beautifully and intricately a gender created in God, by God, for God.

My story is the voice God has given me, and I am going to use it. The growth and expansion of my business and this book, His story, is God's way of getting His word out. We all have a message and a purpose, and it is up to God to show us how to use it.

This book, for me, has been very therapeutic. It's like a final chapter closing as God begins to start a *new* book within me. I am so free of any past pain, anger, and disappointment. There is no bitterness or regret, only love and a desire to please God and do His will.

As much as has been documented, believe it or not, there is so much more that I didn't write about because God didn't lead me to. Maybe there are even some things that He didn't want me to revisit or remember. The bottom line is that what He wanted written and what needs to be heard are within these pages.

Again, this book is a tool and not a weapon. My hurting anyone intentionally is not the will of God, nor would it give His name glory. God placed in me a story of encouragement, power, hope, healing, and promise. Just today, as I was driving along, listening to the radio, I heard a speaker state that it is not intended for us to have God "diffuse" our story and have us forget our past, but purposely for us to allow God to "use" us.

I have come to realize more and more that this healing was for more than just me. The Bible says that perfect love casts out fear. Christ humbled himself, even to death, because He loved us, and when there is love, there is no fear.

Today, wherever you are, no matter what you have gone through or may be going through at this very moment, I want you to set aside that fear. John 3:16 tells us that "God so loved the world that He gave His only begotten son." That means *God loves you*. He knows, hears, and can see everything that you are going through. He was right there when you went through it, and He is here right now. His call to you today is to reach out and accept His extended hand.

You have tried everything else: empty relationships, drugs, sex, and alcohol, but nothing and no one has the power to comfort and save your soul. Nothing and no one can set you free, take away the hurt, harm or pain you have experienced. Nothing and no one can embrace you, fill you with forgiveness and love, and then clean you up like new. Not a single one of them can do these things. Only God can.

The Bible clearly tells us that "Jesus is the way, the truth, and the life." Today, my friend, I want you to make a decision to *choose truth* and begin to live your life. Jesus is the way!

Salvation is a gift, and accepting Jesus is a choice. Romans 10:8-10 gives us direct knowledge and instruction on how to make that choice: It tells us that salvation comes from believing the fact that Jesus, the son of God, died and rose for our sins, "and with the mouth he confesses and confirms his salvation."

I have learned throughout my life that in making the choice to believe in Christ, we *choose life*, but when we firmly make the decision to receive Christ, we *choose to live*. There is a difference. It is time to decide: Are you ready to live?

PRAYER OF SALVATION

Father God, in the name of Jesus, here I am, Your creation, Your child. Lord, You made me by design and You do all things well. No matter how I came here, no matter what I have gone through, it was all a part of Your plan. Lord, I may not understand it, and I may not even like it, but this day I choose to trust You.

I want to know You, I want to hear You, and I want to feel You in my life. This day, I accept Jesus. This day I choose life. I believe that Your son died and rose just for me, and I ask Jesus to come into my heart now. God, I thank You for saving me. I thank You for loving me, and I thank You for now living in me.

***

My dear friend, your life is now changed forever! Don't take it for granted that God heard you. You are now saved, delivered, set free, and healed from all that has hindered you. I could go on and on about the power and greatness of God, but all you have to do, especially when satan comes to try and tell you that nothing has changed, is to remember what I have written within these pages. God has done great works for me, and He is now doing even greater for you. He will never leave you nor forsake you.

My personal desire and prayer is that this book has touched your heart and will be passed on to bless the lives of others.

I would love to hear from you and receive your comments, prayer requests, encouragement and inspiration.

Please feel free to contact me and send comments to
Takiya La'Shaune
PO Box 6221
Beaufort, SC 29903

Or email me at
takiya@takiya-lashaune.com

For bulk and individual book ordering, or to arrange speaking engagements
and women's ministry or social events,
please visit my website at
www.takiya-lashaune.com